VALLEY FORGE TO MONMOUTH
1778

Mark Edward Lender

The U.S. Army Campaigns of the Revolutionary War

Series Editors
David W. Hogan Jr.
Joseph A. Seymour
Jonathan D. Bratten

Opening Shots in the Colonies, 1775–1776
The Canadian Campaign, 1775–1776
The New York Campaign, 1776
The New Jersey Campaign, 1776–1777
The Philadelphia Campaign, 1777
The Saratoga Campaign, 1777
Valley Forge to Monmouth, 1778
The War in the North, 1778–1781
The Frontier War, 1775–1783
The War in the South, 1778–1780
The War in the Carolinas and Georgia, 1781–1782
The War in Virginia, 1781
Securing Victory, 1781–1783

Cover: *Washington Rallying the Troops at Monmouth*, Emanual Gottlieb Leutze, 1857 (*Wikimedia Commons*)

The U.S. Army Campaigns of the Revolutionary War

VALLEY FORGE TO MONMOUTH 1778

by
Mark Edward Lender

Center of Military History
United States Army
Washington, D.C., 2024

Library of Congress Cataloging-in-Publication Data

Names: Lender, Mark Edward, 1947- author. | Center of Military History, issuing body.
Title: Valley Forge to Monmouth, 1778 / by Mark Edward Lender.
Other titles: U.S. Army campaigns of the Revolutionary War.
Description: Washington, D.C. : Center of Military History, United States Army, [2025] | Series:
U.S. Army campaigns of the Revolutionary War | In scope of the U.S. Government
Publishing Office Cataloging and Indexing Program (C&I); Federal Depository Library
Program (FDLP) distribution status to be determined upon publication. | Includes
bibliographical references.
Identifiers: LCCN 2024026146 (print) | LCCN 2024026147 (ebook) | ISBN 9781959302124
(paperback) | ISBN 9781959302124 (Adobe pdf)
Subjects: LCSH: Monmouth, Battle of, Freehold, N.J., 1778. | Valley Forge (Pa.)--History--
Revolution, 1775-1783.
Classification: LCC E263.P4 (print) | LCC E263.P4 (ebook) | DDC 973.3/44--
dc23/eng/20240628 | SUDOC D 114.7/9:V 24
LC record available at https://lccn.loc.gov/2024026146

CMH Pub 71–48

 # CONTENTS

Introduction 7

Strategic Setting 13

Operations 41

Analysis 94

Appendix 111

Bibliographic Note 117

The Author 129

Maps

1. Valley Forge Encampment, Pennsylvania, 19 December 1777–18 June 1778 18
2. Battle of Barren Hill, Pennsylvania, 20 May 1778 47
3. March to Monmouth Courthouse, New Jersey, 15 June 1778 54
4. First Engagement, Battle of Monmouth, 28 June 1778 70

5. British Counterattack, Battle of Monmouth,
    28 June 1778...72
6. The Morass Bridge, Battle of Monmouth,
    28 June 1778...80
7. Continental Counterattacks, Battle of Monmouth,
    28 June 1778 86
8. March to Sandy Hook, New Jersey, 15 June 1778............92

Note: We have retained the original spelling, capitalization, and punctuation in quoted material.

 # INTRODUCTION

As America celebrates the 250th anniversary of the Revolutionary War, it is a perfect time to reflect on the revolutionary generation. In the two-and-a-half centuries since the war, the United States has grappled with the complexities and paradoxes of its revolution. How could a nation be born from the idea that all men are created equal, and yet deny much of that freedom to women and to many of its own population based on the color of their skin? How should a central federal government balance power with state governments? Could those thirteen fractious colonies merge into one nation? The seeds of what would become our country's future political and military conflicts lie in these complexities, as do some of our greatest national accomplishments.

This milestone anniversary is also an appropriate time to reflect on the history of the United States Army. The Army stands as our first truly national institution, having been established by the Continental Congress on 14 June 1775. General George Washington's ability to meld the soldiers of the various colonies together into one national force provided an example to the rest of the country that national unity was possible. If the Army failed to overcome the regional sectionalism prevalent at the time, it would fall to superior British resources and organization. If the Army failed, the nation would fail. Washington gave us the precedent of military subordination to the civil authority, one of the core tenets of our political tradition and way of life. At the end of the war, he resigned his commission and voluntarily gave up all his power to return to civil life. His example has inspired us as a model of military and political leadership for generations.

The Massachusetts militiamen who fired the first shots of the war on 19 April 1775 had no blueprint for creating a nation—nor did many think that the conflict would result in a drive for independence. Deep-seated colonial resentments over their rights as English citizens had been simmering since before the 1750s. As the British Parliament enacted even more restrictive laws, peaceful protests turned to military organization, and finally open violence. As New England formed its Army of Observation in the wake of the battles of Lexington and Concord, the Continental Congress saw the need for a national army.

For eight long years, the Continental Army maintained itself in the field, despite fighting superior odds, starvation, diminished resources, and divided leadership. Setbacks in the New York Campaign of 1776 nearly destroyed Washington's army as the British drove it into Pennsylvania. Yet as 1777 opened, Washington changed the operational situation by seizing the initiative in a series of tactical victories at Trenton and Princeton, New Jersey. That fall, a British invasion into northern New York met with failure and capture at the hands of the Northern Army and militia at Saratoga, ultimately bringing France into war on the side of the United States. At the same time, Washington kept a British army penned up in Philadelphia while he instituted a training regimen for his army at their encampment in Valley Forge that winter. Trained under the tutelage of German-born Frederick von Steuben, the Continentals harried the British out of Philadelphia and back to New York City, fighting like regulars at Monmouth in 1778.

General Washington faced the challenge of countering British victories at Charleston, South Carolina, and Savannah, Georgia, when the British shifted the war south in 1780, while also containing powerful British forces in Canada and New York City. Relying on skilled subordinates such as Anthony Wayne, Nathanael Greene, and the Marquis de Lafayette—all of whom in turn worked closely with state militia—Washington was able to hold the delicate balance of power in both the northern and southern theaters. Seizing the opportunity presented by his French allies, Washington quickly shifted a large portion of his army from New York City to Yorktown,

Virginia. There, the allies laid siege to another British army, forcing it to capitulate in the fall of 1781. Although this victory sounded the death knell for British control of the American colonies, peace talks would last for two more years. During this time, Washington kept an army in the field, maintained the supremacy of civil authority over the military, and presented a credible threat to the remaining British garrisons. When the peace came, the true architects of the revolution's success were the Continental Army, state troops, and the militia.

The Revolutionary War created the model for our modern Army. It set the stage for what eventually would become a three-component force, with the Continentals and militia operating in complementary roles. Today, thirty-three National Guard units can trace their lineage to the Revolutionary War, which is a testament to their role in the formation of this country. Eight army branches also have their beginnings in the revolution. The U.S. Army's very motto, "This We'll Defend," is rooted in the "self-evident" truths enunciated in the Declaration of Independence and American interpretations of Enlightenment traditions, which came together in the seal for the Board of War and Ordnance and became the Department of the Army seal in the twentieth century. Unfortunately, it also would take until the twentieth century for the U.S. Army to be as racially integrated as its Continental Army forebears.

The traditions begun and precedents set by Washington and his soldiers continue to influence the U.S. Army and causes around the world. The seeds of hope shown at Trenton and Princeton have inspired leaders in other dark times, such as Bull Run, Shiloh, and Kasserine Pass. The revolutionary generation taught us that the true strength of our Army is our people; from the frontline soldiers to the camp followers who sustained the regiments. And it is to these individuals, who forged ahead through privation and misery to final victory and who rarely received any greater recognition in their own lifetimes than the simple epitaph "A Soldier of the Revolution," that these volumes are humbly dedicated.

CHARLES R. BOWERY JR.
Executive Director

VALLEY FORGE TO MONMOUTH 1778

In late May 1778, General George Washington, having survived the winter in Valley Forge, Pennsylvania, took some spare minutes to write an old Virginia friend, Landon Carter. Like Washington, Carter stood high in the Old Dominion's social elite. The letter, the kind one wrote only to someone close and trusted, discussed personal matters and brought Carter up to date on the military situation. Washington was upbeat, but he unburdened himself on the searing Valley Forge experience. Only the "constant interposition" of "Providence," he assured Carter, had sustained the army through its ordeal. Washington also related the political fire he had confronted as some officers and political figures maneuvered to curtail his authority as commander in chief—the so-called Conway Cabal. Nevertheless, prospects had "miraculously brightened," he was relieved to note, as efforts to resupply, retrain, reorganize, and reequip the Continentals took hold. The new Franco-American alliance seemed like manna from heaven. Things were looking up

Yet the general still worried. In particular, the strategic outlook was cloudy. Washington was sure the British would evacuate Philadelphia, Pennsylvania, but he told Carter he did not know when

George Washington, Charles Willson Peale, 1777 (*Permanent Art Collection of West Chester University of Pennsylvania*)

or what to do about it. He was certain the enemy would head for New York City. But would they go by water? March overland across New Jersey? And if the British marched, could he stop them? From all of this, Carter gathered that Washington's army had borne much and had a great deal more in front of it.

Although the missive to Carter was a private communication, it was one of the best situation reports Washington ever had penned. It traced the trajectory from the tribulations at Valley Forge to the army's springtime recovery and the advent of a new campaign. That new campaign would be brief (roughly five weeks) but critical. It would begin with operations around Valley Forge in late May, continue with the British evacuation of Philadelphia on 18 June, and ten days later culminate in one of the war's longest days of action at the Battle of Monmouth in Monmouth County, New Jersey. That series of actions would pit an experienced British army under Lt. Gen. Sir Henry Clinton, a veteran commander, against a Continental Army and a general largely untested since the Valley Forge encampment. The campaign would try the mettle of both armies and test the determination of the rival commanders in one of the most dramatic chapters in America's founding struggle.

STRATEGIC SETTING

The early winter of 1777 found the Revolutionary War in something of a hiatus. In occupied Philadelphia, the royal commander in chief, Lt. Gen. Sir William Howe, was at a loss. Tactically, he had done well. He had brought his army by sea from New York in August 1777 and bested Washington in every confrontation; in September, he took the de facto rebel capital of Philadelphia without a fight. By the end of November, he had driven the patriots from Forts Mifflin and Mercer on the Pennsylvania and New Jersey banks of the Delaware River, enabling the *Royal Navy* to supply his army in the city. It was an impressive performance.

Nevertheless, the British war effort had failed in 1777. Lt. Gen. John Burgoyne's army had surrendered at Saratoga, New York, in October, and Howe would spend years trying to explain why, instead of moving up the Hudson River to link up with Burgoyne, he had pursued a showdown with Washington around Philadelphia. Howe's campaign, however successful tactically, had been a strategic fiasco. He had failed to destroy the Continental Army, the revolution lived on, and his political masters were not pleased.

Howe had no answer for a stalemated war; he had no strategic vision to replace the plans of 1777. To the immense frustration of many of his subordinates, he had discounted a winter offensive. His army had suffered losses approaching 20 percent, and London was in no hurry to send major reinforcements. He had enough troops to hold the city and to conduct foraging operations in Pennsylvania and New Jersey and even to launch occasional raids on rebel units. He also fortified Billingsport on the New Jersey banks of the Delaware. Yet Howe believed a strike at Valley Forge was too risky, and even foraging missions frequently ran into trouble. The Pennsylvania militia patrolled the roads out of Philadelphia, and British forays often met with militia and Continental harassment. Indeed, even though Washington's exhausted troops were incapable of major offensive operations, they were not inactive. Over the winter and into the spring of 1778, the overall situation was inconclusive—a state of affairs hardly to Great Britain's advantage.

Howe endured another disappointment. He had assumed thousands of loyalists would rally to the king's colors. Yet, by early 1778, the eleven loyalist units enlisted from Philadelphia and neighboring Maryland and New Jersey counted fewer than 2,500 troops—hardly a recruiting groundswell. The general had courted the city's social elite, but most Tories never felt secure enough to show their political colors without direct redcoat support. With his invasion having failed in military and political terms, in October 1777 the disillusioned army commander had written to London asking to resign. By the early weeks of 1778, Howe, awaiting relief, had received no new instructions from Lord George Germain, the American secretary and the cabinet minister most responsible for the war effort. For the time being, British military affairs were adrift.

The 1777 campaign had ended on a whimper. In early December, Washington, frustrated after the succession of defeats and not sure of British intentions—would Howe press his advantage and come after the exhausted Continentals?—had pulled back to defensive ground in the Whitemarsh, Pennsylvania, area, some 16 miles north of Philadelphia. There, between 5 and 8 December, the British probed his lines, but Washington refused to be drawn into a general action. Disappointed, Howe retired to the city for the winter. Although there was no real battle, the engagement in Whitemarsh was instructive. It demonstrated that the battered Continentals could still fight and remained dangerous. Although accounts of numbers vary widely, Washington had about 10,000 effectives (individuals considered part of fighting units) at Whitemarsh, easily as many as Howe. In days, the rebels would march to winter quarters at Valley Forge, still an effective army. In breaking off after Whitemarsh, Howe tacitly conceded that the Continentals were a foe of near-equivalent strength.

If the campaign was a disappointment for Washington, his problems were monumentally different from Howe's. Among patriots, there was political pressure to keep fighting, and Pennsylvanians in particular clamored for the recovery of Philadelphia. Nevertheless, with his ranks exhausted and logistics in disarray, Washington informed Congress that offensive operations were impossible. Usually tactful with civilian authorities, in this case he was blunt. "It would give me infinite pleasure to afford protection to every individual and to every Spot of Ground in the whole of the United States," the general wrote to South Carolinian Henry Laurens, the recently elected president of Congress. "Nothing is more my wish. But this is not possible with our present force." There would be no winter offensive.

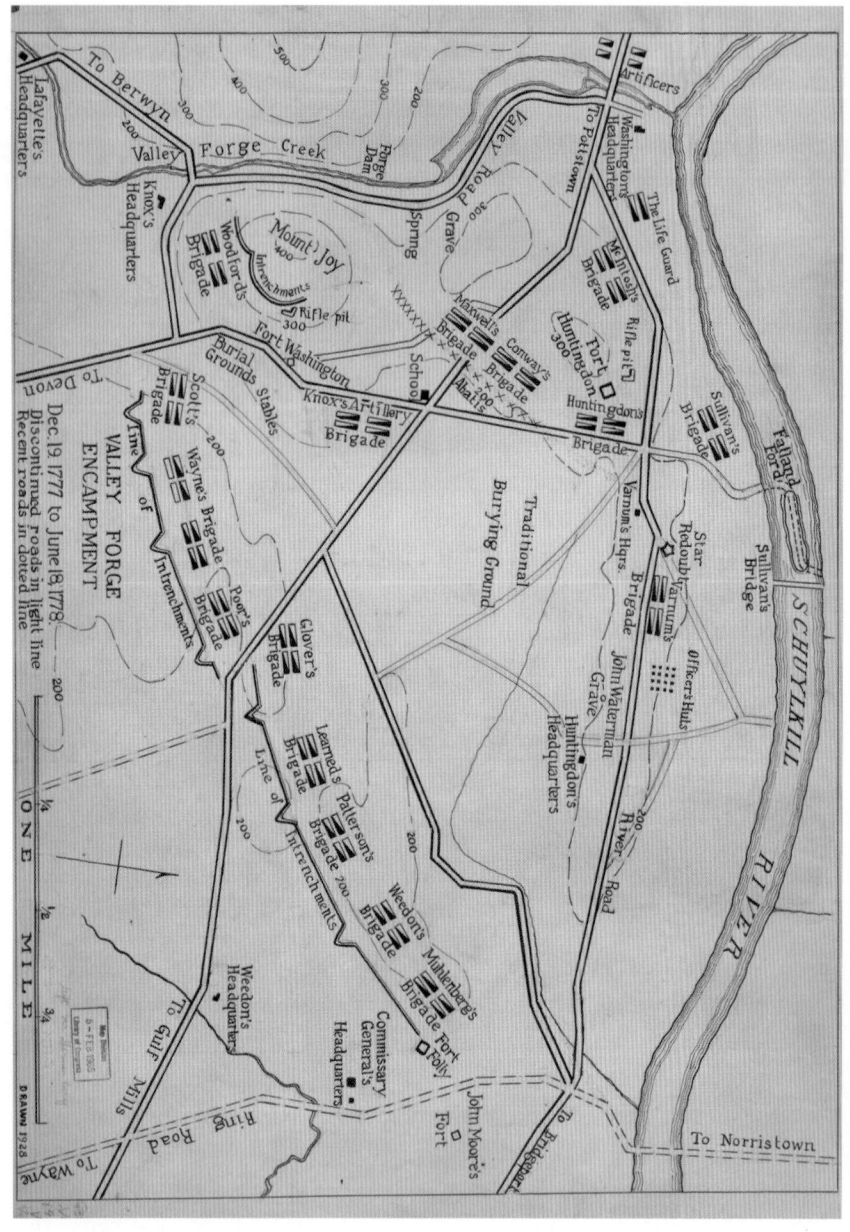

Valley Forge Encampment, Dec. 19, 1777 to June 18, 1778, cartographer unknown, 1928 (*Library of Congress*)

Winter at Valley Forge

Instead, on 19 December, the general led his army to winter quarters. Where to go had engendered debate. Some officers favored Wilmington, Delaware; others wanted more westerly Pennsylvania positions ranging between Reading and Lancaster. However, as opposed to other locations, Valley Forge enjoyed some key advantages. The site was 18 miles northwest of Philadelphia—a bit farther by road. It was home to a small patriot supply depot, albeit one that the British had raided the previous September. Yet even though Howe was familiar with the area, Valley Forge was far enough from Philadelphia to make any British surprise unlikely. It was also close enough for Washington to keep an eye on Howe and to take advantage of any chance opportunities. In case the British did attack, Valley Forge was defensible.

With the protection of the Schuylkill River to the north, the encampment had high terrain to the west on Mount Joy and Mount Misery. Soon after arrival, the troops began preparing entrenchments and larger fortifications around the camp perimeter. They also bridged the Schuylkill, which would allow rapid movement northward if necessary. Thus, the main army enjoyed relatively secure ground for the winter (*Map 1*). Washington also sent two brigades with Brig. Gen. William Smallwood to Wilmington and most of the Continental cavalry to Trenton, New Jersey.

However, Washington never intended Valley Forge as an exclusively defensive position. As 1778 dawned, the strategic outlook for the Americans was gloomy but not impossible, and Washington intended to keep fighting, albeit at a lower level. To ensure popular support for the revolution, the army needed to demonstrate that it remained effective. The commander in chief wanted to interdict British foraging and security operations outside of the city. If it accomplished nothing else, such activity at least would keep Howe guessing about patriot capabilities and intensions. Washington also was keen to prevent illicit civilian trade with the enemy and to offer protection to regional farmers, whose crops, forage, and livestock were essential to army supply. Small-unit actions began

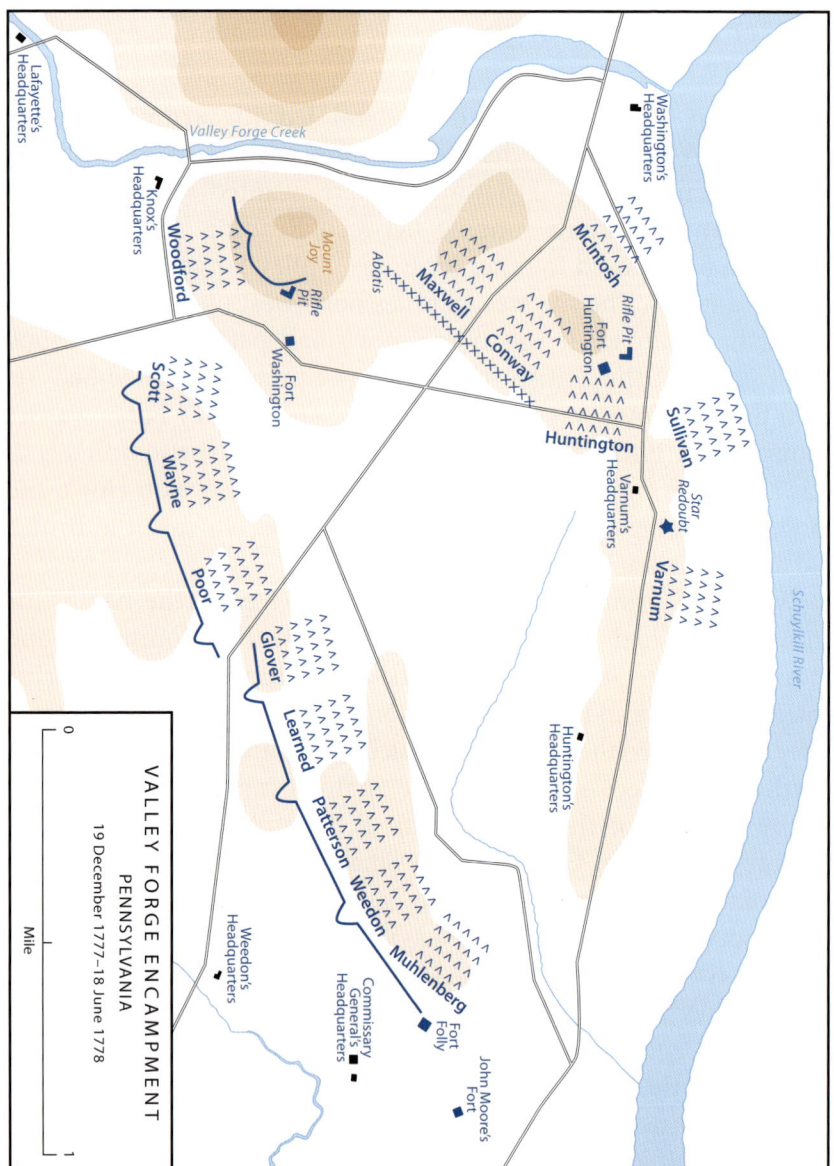

Map 1

only days after marching to Valley Forge. As early as 22 December, Continentals under Col. Daniel Morgan tangled with a British foraging party. As the rebels and British actively patrolled, such incidents were repeated through the winter and early spring. Even in a weakened state, the rebels could still sting if given an opportunity. In particular, Continental dragoons under Capt. Henry "Light-Horse Harry" Lee III (father of Robert E. Lee; promoted to major in April 1778) became the scourge of British foragers. Lee never fought a major action, but he forced the British to commit significant resources to security efforts—a worthy objective in and of itself. Such operations routinely kept sizable numbers of troops out of camp. As much as a winter encampment, then, Valley Forge was also a forward operating base. The Continental Army, even as it endured a hard winter, was never inert.

In fact, Valley Forge was a hive of activity when troops were not on active operations. It was a large cantonment. With at least 12,000 troops, but maybe as many as 19,000, and a varying number of camp followers, the encampment was 2 miles long and 2¼ miles wide. As the army settled in for the winter, Valley Forge took on aspects of urban life. The camp ranked only behind Philadelphia, New York, and Boston, Massachusetts, as the largest "city" in the rebellious colonies. During the early weeks, the troops labored to erect huts against the cold, and the results were impressive: camp fortifications eventually enclosed around 1,500 log huts laid out roughly—sometimes *very* roughly—in "streets." Like any busy town, Valley Forge had to cope with issues of sanitation, medical care, and public order; and it had to interact with its surrounding neighbors, including civilians fleeing the turbulence around Philadelphia. The encampment attracted civilian visitors, and commissary officials encouraged regional farmers to sell any available produce at camp markets. Many residents were Quakers who wanted no part of the war. Some members of this religious group were quiet loyalists—and Washington did lock up several he considered security risks—but others volunteered to come to the camp to nurse the sick. By and large, whatever their political sentiments, the locals gave the army little trouble, which was a boon for camp security.

Valley Forge also had its own civilian elements, usually termed camp followers. Commissary personnel, civilians in Continental pay, were a constant presence, as were various teamsters and contractors, civilian artificers, laborers, and even some servants and enslaved people who were attached to officers. In January 1778, general orders allowed each brigade a sutler who could sell liquor, tobacco, and soap at set prices, "but no other articles . . . on any pretence whatever." Sutlers apparently did not honor this last regulation, except, perhaps, in the breach. Otherwise, they sold whatever they could at whatever prices camp residents were willing to pay, and they even constructed semipermanent structures in which to store their wares and conduct business. The army's Valley Forge tribulations did not extinguish the entrepreneurial spirit.

The military community at Valley Forge included about 400 women and children. This was to be expected, as women were a normal part of eighteenth-century armies, and some rank and file would not have enlisted if they could not have brought their wives or consorts along. Washington initially frowned on women accompanying the troops, fearing they would slow movements and be the source of disorder, but he soon conceded they were essential to camp routine. Some were wives of senior officers, including Martha D. C. Washington, who billeted in relative comfort in private residences. In contrast, most of the women, having little to sustain them in civilian life, shared the hardships of the enlisted soldiers while serving as nurses (entitled to army rations), cooks, laundresses, seamstresses, foragers, herders, and general helpmates. Some were in business, probably illegally, as sutlers. While most of the women lived relatively anonymous lives as camp followers, some took on greater roles. One of them, Mary Ludwig Hays, would make a name for herself later in the war at Monmouth Courthouse.

This record of camp activity was remarkable given the severe tribulations of that winter; indeed, they became central to the republic's founding myth. When Washington had told Laurens there could be no winter offensive, the general had not exaggerated the condition of his army. Even with basic shelter secured, supplies became scarce. On 23 December, the general told Laurens that the Commissary Department, responsible for securing food, forage, and clothing, was not up to the job. Consequently, he warned, "I

Return of the Scout to Valley Forge, Snow-swept Winter Camp, c. 1777, Harrington Fitzgerald, ca. 1880–1910 (*Library of Congress*)

am now convinced . . . that unless some great and capital change suddenly takes place in that line this Army must inevitably be reduced to one or other of these three things. Starve—dissolve—or disperse, in order to obtain subsistence in the best manner they can."

But was the situation really that bad? In considering Washington's letter to Laurens, a few modern historians have expressed a bit of skepticism, arguing that the general wanted the letter to spur congressional action on the army's behalf. They point to the facts that, in late December, the army remained operational and commissary records indicate that rations remained adequate. This perspective has the benefit of 250 years of hindsight, though, and goes too far in suggesting that Washington deliberately was misleading Congress. It is just as plausible that Washington had considered the dire situation at Valley Forge honestly and was not, in his mind, exaggerating. He was not alone. In late December and early January, other officers noted the distressing lack of blankets and clothing, and there genuinely were instances of soldiers leaving "bloody footprints" in the snow. Things became even worse as the winter deepened. On 16 February, Massachusetts congressional delegate Francis Dana, then visiting Valley Forge, informed his colleagues that a regiment had risen in protest, marched on their general's headquarters, and "laid before him their complaints, and threatened to quit the army." It was all Maj. Gen. John Paterson could do to placate the troops. But, Dana warned, the "same spirit" was rising in the rest of the army. More than once, angry soldiers protested meager rations and teetered on the edge of mutiny. One commissary officer, cornered by cold and hungry Continentals, reported that he was afraid for his life. Washington's army was in real trouble.

This was tragic. Too many of the patriots' war efforts suffered from self-inflicted wounds. Supply operations broke down not only in the face of repeated defeats, but also from bungled administrative efforts. The chief problem was maintaining transportation to enable deliveries to the army. Stores existed in scattered locations, poor recordkeeping prevented a clear understanding of stores on hand, and political ineptitude made things worse. When the quartermaster general, Maj. Gen. Thomas Mifflin, resigned, pleading ill health (although he remained politically active), Congress showed no urgency in naming a replacement.

The delegates also fumbled commissary operations. In 1776, Congress had assigned a group of its members to the Board of War, which was designed to relieve Washington of the more mundane and time-consuming aspects of army administration: routine correspondence and recordkeeping, dealing with prisoners of war, and storing equipment not in active use. Congress never intended for the board to be involved in daily army management or in operational or strategic matters. In October 1777, however, under Mifflin's guidance, Congress reorganized the board, replacing busy delegates with outside appointees with supposed expertise in military administration.

The new board included Mifflin and, as of January 1778, at Mifflin's strong suggestion, Maj. Gen. Horatio L. Gates, the popular victor of the Battles of Saratoga, became board president. Both Gates and Mifflin had strained relations with Washington. Mifflin, a longtime patriot and an active Pennsylvania politico, had been a close aide to the commander in chief early in the war. His faith in Washington faltered, however, with the defeats of 1776. Their relationship further cooled as Mifflin resented Washington's growing reliance on Nathanael Greene and as Washington came to question Mifflin's problematic performance as quartermaster general. Gates, a British veteran who settled in Virginia after serving in the Seven Years' War, was also an early patriot. He worked closely with Washington at the beginning of the war, bringing vitally needed administrative skills to the new patriot army. He was no military lightweight, but he intrigued frequently in Congress seeking influence and choice commands. After Saratoga, he was a genuine hero, and he basked in the flattery of politicians and officers who honestly thought the war effort might do better in his hands than in Washington's. Mifflin and Gates certainly thought so.

In a classic case of what today would be called "mission creep," the Board of War actively sought to expand its authority into key army functions. The impact on commissary operations, in particular, was tragic. At the board's urging, Congress approved a reform of commissary efforts. Instead of firing the ineffectual commissary general—an officer Washington badly wanted to replace—the delegates allowed the board to appoint superintendents to compete with Commissary Department purchasing agents. Congress specified that these new officers were not responsible to Washington; they would report to the board. At the same time, Pennsylvania, in a well-intentioned effort, also sent purchasing agents into the field—so that three uncoordinated procurement efforts now competed for the same supplies of food and forage. It was an administrative nightmare at a time when unity of command should have been the priority. Although Congress could do little to alleviate the financial woes that left most of the army unpaid for three months—it simply did not have enough money—but there was no excuse for its lack of attention to the administrative mess that left the army desperately short of human and animal sustenance.

Problematic supply operations compelled unceasing attention at headquarters. Washington corresponded with governors and other authorities, urging them to straighten out supply bottlenecks and to procure food, forage, salt, wagons, liquor, livestock, and other necessities and services for their Continental regiments—all with mixed results. Initially afraid of alienating civilian support, the general had shied away from impressing produce and other supplies from regional inhabitants. However, as early as November 1777, he resorted to this method after Congress pressed him on the matter. In issuing an order to collect blankets, clothing, and shoes from Pennsylvania civilians, Washington reminded his officers that "in doing this [they were] to take Care . . . [that anyone] Notoriously disaffected to the Cause of American Liberty [does] not escape [their] Vigilance." One of the most dramatic steps was the "Grand Forage," which the Continentals staged during February and March. With food and forage dangerously low, Washington tasked the competent Maj. Gen. Nathanael Greene with leading 1,500 soldiers in a sweep of farms in Pennsylvania, Maryland, Delaware, and western New Jersey. The operation was something of a paradox: The army was close to starvation, but it still was able to execute a broad-ranging mission. The patriot units gathered enough supplies to stave off serious hunger among troops and animals while frustrating British efforts to intercept them. Hungry soldiers can be highly motivated.

There were other problems. The weather did not help, though it was relatively mild compared to later in the war—the brutal winter of 1779–1780 in Morristown, Pennsylvania, was much worse—and the cold at Valley Forge was no more than many eighteenth-century armies endured. Still, road conditions alternated between snow and slush, impeding deliveries and periodically reducing the soldiery to borderline starvation. Over the winter, weakened through prolonged adversity, more than 2,000 troops (and, one assumes, many camp followers) succumbed to camp diseases—usually typhoid, dysentery, smallpox, and other fevers. For many soldiers, it was too much. Desertion rates of 20 percent were common, and some regiments recorded losses of 50 percent. The numbers tell the tale: In November 1777, the general had 19,415 personnel present and fit for duty; by March 1778, there were only 7,316 (although, again, there are differing opinions on troop strength). Nor were all officers dependable. Perceived civilian neglect of the army and arguments with Congress over postwar pensions and matters of seniority and promotion shook the morale of the officer corps. The many resignations, requests for leave, and unexcused absences from officers facing financial ruin drove Washington to distraction. The loss of officers, he fumed, "will shake the very existence of the Army."

Washington equally was upset by criticisms of his leadership and, as he later confided to Landon Carter, by what he believed was a threat to his job. Censure of Washington's generalship was no surprise. Historically, it was common to sack losing generals, as the British had done repeatedly during the Seven Years' War, and patriots were well aware of these precedents. As early as late 1776, there were doubts about Washington. Adjutant General Joseph Reed and, most notably, Maj. Gen. Charles Lee, the army's second-ranking officer, groused indiscreetly at Washington's performance. Worse followed in 1777. The defeats around Philadelphia stood in bold relief against Gates's victory at Saratoga, and they triggered comparisons between the two generals that did not flatter Washington.

Washington's critics jelled loosely in what became known among nineteenth-century historians as the Conway Cabal—although there was never an organized plot—in which disaffected patriots toyed with the idea of trading Washington for Gates. Thomas Conway, Irish-born but raised in France, was one of the many French volunteers in Continental service. He was a competent brigadier, and he was diligent in training his brigade. The British considered him clever. Conway gravitated to the orbit of Washington's opponents, especially Mifflin and Gates, when Washington opposed his promotion to major general ahead of more senior Continental brigadiers—which, in fact, meant every other Continental brigadier, as Conway was junior to all of them. Washington previously had refrained from responding to such rumblings of dissent, but when he learned of a letter from Conway to Gates lauding Gates and castigating Washington, he confronted both generals. Publicly embarrassed, Gates and Conway abjectly disclaimed animosity toward their commander in chief, and the rest of Washington's critics fell into uncomfortable silence. Nevertheless, however inchoate the general's critics may have been, there were legitimate questions about his military record—questions that remained to be answered.

From a Fighting Force to a Continental Army

Just as the Valley Forge winter was an epic of survival, it also became a narrative of revival. By January, the critical supply situation finally spurred Congress to act. It dispatched a committee to Valley Forge to work with Washington to resolve the crisis, with the commander in chief setting the agenda. The group's reports of bureaucratic bottlenecks, suffering soldiers, angry officers, and Washington's efforts to hold everything together appalled the delegates. Congressional surprise at the state of affairs at Valley Forge was inexcusable, but, confronted with stark realities reported by their own committee, the delegates moved to remedy the situation.

Significantly, Congress got rid of the Board of War's superintendents and agreed to new appointments and funding for the existing Commissary and Quartermaster Departments. In early March 1778, Greene agreed to serve as quartermaster general. Longing for martial glory, he loathed giving up division command. "No body ever heard of a quarter Master in History," he lamented.

Only Washington's entreaties persuaded him to take the job. Soon after, Connecticut's capable Jeremiah Wadsworth took over as commissary general of purchases. Wadsworth, who had made a fortune in the West Indies trade, had an extensive background in state military procurement. He was a friend of Greene's, but, unlike the major general, Wadsworth never asked where commissaries stood in history.

Posterity, however, would laud the roles of both of these exceptional men. Greene and Wadsworth spent freely. Although Congress winced at their accounts, they demonstrated the fiscal truism that knowing *how* to spend money was as important as having money to spend. They jump-started logistics operations, improving transportation services that enabled deliveries of food, clothing, forage, camp implements, and munitions. Greene and Wadsworth enjoyed considerable good fortune: Washington lent his full

Nathanael Greene (1742–1786), John Trumbull, 1792 (*Courtesy of the Trumbull Collection, Yale University Art Gallery, Yale University, New Haven, CT*)

support, the weather moderated after February, and even the British cooperated by not attacking Valley Forge. The two department heads were diligent, and they deserved much of the credit for the improving state of the army.

As logistics improved, the commander in chief addressed the critical issues of recruiting, army reorganization, and training. Even a well-supplied army was useless unless it could perform in the field, and Washington understood his regulars lacked British tactical skills. Before 1778, training had taken place largely at the company and regimental levels (although some brigades did train as complete units), but not all officers employed the same regimen. The army took tentative steps toward uniform drill in 1777, but active operations had prevented Washington from implementing a standard system. The rebel chief considered the matter pressing, and he wanted an inspector general to implement a uniform tactical and training program. In late 1777, he had proposed as much to Congress, specifying that the new inspector general would be a senior member of his staff. The Board of War, however, guided by the former quartermaster general, General Mifflin, convinced Congress otherwise—thus precipitating a perplexing controversy between Washington and his political masters.

In December 1777, Congress approved the establishment of two inspector generals, though ultimately it would appoint only one. Instead of serving as staff officers under the commander in chief, the inspectors would be creatures of the Board of War and independent of Washington. They would implement regulations devised by the board, and Washington would lose the power even to evaluate his own subordinates. For Washington, the congressional action was ominous. "Taken to its logical conclusions," the official history of the Army's inspector generals has observed, the arrangement "would have effectively eliminated the command authority of the Commander in Chief." Washington was furious at what he considered a personal affront—compounded by the promotion of Thomas Conway to major general and his appointment as the new inspector general. Conway actively had importuned Congress for promotion over the army's senior brigadiers. Most of the officer corps loathed him, and when he appeared at Valley Forge, Washington was barely civil. Frozen out by the commander in chief and the officer corps, Conway rode back to Congress and complained. The perplexed delegates did nothing in response. For the time being, Conway technically remained inspector general, but he never functioned as such.

Jeremiah Wadsworth, John Angel James Wilcox, 1776 *(Connecticut Historical Society)*

Still, the Continentals needed an effective inspector general, and everyone knew it. Luckily—and unexpectedly—the right man arrived seemingly from out of the blue. This was Friedrich Wilhelm Ludolf Gerhard Augustin von Steuben, a Prussian military instructor of considerable experience. Steuben had joined the Prussian army as a teenager and, as a junior officer, had spent a decade training troops. He served gallantly in the Seven Years' War, in which he gained valuable staff experience and an appreciation of light infantry tactics. Beginning in 1762, Captain Steuben served two years as an aide to Prussian monarch Frederick II (commonly known as Frederick the Great), an "assignment [that] provided him with the best staff training available in the eighteenth century." Late in life, Steuben claimed that army politics forced his retirement, although many officers found themselves unemployed when Prussia reduced its forces at the end of the war in 1763. Steuben then found a position as *Hofmarschall* (chamberlain) to a minor German noble, Prince Josef Friedrich Wilhelm of Hohenzollern-Hechingen. He left Josef in 1777, in debt and under hazy circumstances, vainly seeking a post in a European army. Disappointed, he then approached, through intermediaries, the American commissioners in Paris, France, sounding them out on employment in the Continental Army—and his luck changed.

The commissioners were impressed. Benjamin Franklin, probably hoping to smooth Steuben's way with Congress, inflated the former captain's résumé—calling him a Prussian lieutenant general. In any event, Steuben made a good impression in America. He never badgered Congress for senior rank; rather, he agreed to serve as a volunteer inspector general. He left discussions of permanent post and rank for later, with the understanding that if he proved himself in this first position, appropriate rewards would follow.

Steuben went to work with a will. He knew how to train and motivate soldiers, and he knew he had to prepare the Continentals to face veteran British regulars. The redcoats were formidable infantry. They were the heart of the king's army, products of a regimen that offered little on theoretical aspects of war, but emphasized strict discipline, the repetition of drill and tactical evolutions, and the practical aspects of soldiering and military organization. By the 1770s, recruits learned drill largely from British adjutant general Edward Harvey's *The Manual Exercise, as Ordered by His Majesty in 1764*, popularly known as "*The '64*." Individual regiments, however, often adapted *The '64* to local circumstances or to the preferences of commanding officers or other training publications.

Harvey's drill, including the manual of arms, was demanding. There were twenty steps and forty-two separate motions, including firing, between the first instruction ("Poise Your Firelock!") and the last ("Secure Your Firelock!"). There were additional commands for marching, dressing ranks, firing by platoons, bayonet assaults, moving from column to line, and more. Instruction was the province of noncommissioned officers, and proficiency came only through

Washington at Valley Forge, E. Percy Moran, ca. 1911 (*Library of Congress*)

repeated drill and long experience. Much of that experience, and certainly maneuvers at the regimental level, came on campaign, as the regiments generally were dispersed in peacetime and seldom trained as a whole. In fact, of the redcoats facing Washington in early 1778, probably only 25 percent had trained as part of a full regiment before shipping out to America—where they continued to drill "endlessly, and of necessity." From the individual soldier to the regimental level, it was largely the regimen of *The '64* and constant practice under an "officer corps which was careerist, . . . long-serving, . . . notably experienced, . . . and capable" that made the British army an effective force. This was the standard the Prussian officer would have to match.

Steuben knew all of this. He also knew as he shaped his plans that he would not have to start from scratch. In early 1778, the Continental Army was not a mob; the veteran troops had a working knowledge of maneuver and weapons drill, and many officers (including some veterans of the Seven Years' War) were familiar with European military ideas, including the very publications their British counterparts were reading. Harvey's manual was widely available, as were British Maj. Gen. Humphrey Bland's *A Treatise of Military Discipline* and other titles on drill and tactics. Indeed, Johann Ewald, a jaeger (rifleman) captain campaigning with Howe, was impressed to find how well-read the patriot officers were. Rebel officers drilled their regiments to any number of these regimens. Steuben's task lay in designing what Washington insisted upon: a uniform training program with a standardized manual of arms and tactical evolutions.

The baron—Steuben had assumed the title *Freiherr* (baron) in Europe, and patriots never begrudged it—knew he could not simply adopt an existing training regimen. Recalling his thinking on the matter, he wrote Franklin in 1779 that "circumstances obliged me to deviate from the Principles adopted in the European Armies." The slow pace of European systems and their complicated nature were a poor fit for Americans. Most patriots had far less formal military traditions, their understanding of combat derived largely from long-standing militia practices. Moreover, the rebels were less suited for a drill-and-command regimen linked to the rigid social hierarchies of the Old World. Rather, Steuben called on his knowledge of American practices and the various British and European drills to devise a largely new regimen. He began by simplifying British drill, significantly reducing, for example, the number of steps and motions in the manual of arms, to allow for faster loading and firing. He increased the British cadence of sixty steps per minute to the Prussian standard of seventy-five, and he eliminated movements in single file in favor of columns of four, which allowed for faster and more compact maneuvers. Steuben carefully detailed the steps in moving from column to line and back again, a proficiency essential to success in combat. The Continentals learned or relearned volley fire, skirmishing operations, and any number of other tactical evolutions, all according to a new uniform regimen. Bayonet drill imparted to the patriots proficiency with the weapon the British had been using to deadly effect. Steuben taught a brutal trade, but under his tutelage, the army was shaping up.

Steuben enjoyed Washington's full support. The commander in chief provided troops for a model company, which Steuben drilled as an example for the rest of the army. Subinspectors, learning from the model company, then drilled the regiments and brigades. By the late spring, the new training extended even to detached units, such as the New Jersey Brigade operating in its home territory. Breaking with European practice, Steuben insisted officers personally instruct their troops or at least supervise experienced noncommissioned officers who also trained recruits. Either way, officers were responsible for the proficiency of their units. Washington approved the publication of Steuben's various lessons for dissemination throughout the officer corps. The commander in chief and his generals carefully reviewed each lesson, sometimes suggesting a change. Reflecting the American preference for marksmanship over unaimed volley fire—the European tradition—they changed the baron's old-style command of "Present!" to "Take Aim!" preceding the command to "Fire!" They approved Steuben's many recommendations on matters of camp sanitation, uniform recordkeeping, and regular inspections. The Prussian was nothing if not thorough. In 1779, the army compiled, edited, and published the lessons as Steuben's *Regulations for the Order and Discipline of the Troops of the United States*, which soon became better known as the "Blue Book" because of the color of its cover.

For the most part, the army was grateful for Steuben's work. When some brigade commanders grumbled that Steuben had overstepped his authority and was impinging on their prerogatives, Washington rejected their complaints. The commander in chief tolerated no deviations from Steuben's instruction; failure to conform, he warned, would "again plunge the Army into that Contrariety and Confusion from which it is endeavouring to emerge." By the end of the winter, training extended to brigade-level maneuvers, and the Continental Line had made significant strides toward professionalism. With Washington's enthusiastic endorsement, Congress eventually confirmed Steuben as inspector general with the rank of major general. Steuben was never a miracle worker at Valley Forge; he did not have to be. He was a professional working with good troops, and that was enough.

As Steuben standardized training, Washington and his officers addressed other pressing issues. The commander in chief took a direct role in reorganizing the infantry. As in the British military, the foot regiments were the army's backbone, and Washington moved vigorously to replenish the depleted ranks. With congressional authorization, he began reducing the number of regiments from 104 to 80, consolidating weaker units into fewer but stronger outfits. Even a goal of eighty regiments was ambitious, but at least it was more realistic. He pushed the states to pursue enlistments. To meet troop quotas, states offered supplemental bounties to volunteers and exemptions from militia duty to those who hired substitutes for Continental service. In some cases, they even conscripted new soldiers from existing militia ranks. New Hampshire and Massachusetts led the way in 1777, and New Jersey and Maryland followed the year after. By May 1778, the Continental ranks had risen to more than 15,000.

The army reforming at Valley Forge was a study in ethnic diversity—one modern study has aptly deemed it "a cosmopolitan community." White soldiers, who made up about 90 percent of the army, were a broad mix of Scotch-Irish, English, Irish, German, Dutch, and others with European roots, many of them recent immigrants. The remaining soldiers were people of color, most of whom were Black, and some of whom were American Indians. There were a few Mahican American Indians from Stockbridge, Massachusetts, already at camp, when, in mid-May 1778, forty-seven Oneida and possibly Tuscarora volunteers arrived. Early in the war, Congress had barred non-White enlistments, with Southerners particularly opposed to arming Black people. But, by late 1777, troop shortages had become acute, and opposition to African American recruits had faded. (South Carolina and Georgia, however, never allowed Black people to serve in their Continental regiments.)

How many Black and Indian troops were at Valley Forge? Precise figures are unavailable, but there is some revealing documentation. On 24 August 1778, almost two months to the day after the Battle of Monmouth, an army roster specifically identified Black (and presumably Indian) soldiers in the twelve brigades under Washington's immediate command. There were 755—roughly 10 percent of Washington's 7,600 soldiers—who were listed as fit for duty. This total did not include sick troops, those on detached duty,

Drawing of a Mahican American Indian from Stockbridge, Massachusetts, Johann von Ewald, 1778 (*Wikimedia Commons*)

or those who otherwise were not with the main army. In particular, some Virginia units and the four regiments (about 900 soldiers) of the New Jersey Brigade were not included in the August return. Additional sources account for these formations, which in turn increase the estimated total number of Black and American Indian soldiers to at least 880. Whatever the exact numbers, it is clear that the army that endured Valley Forge and later marched to Monmouth Courthouse was a racially and ethnically integrated force. Although there were no Black officers, there is no indication of serious racial animosities among the troops.

As the army rebuilt its ranks and reorganized, it also reequipped. Over the early spring, shipments of French muskets began arriving in camp, though there were not enough to arm all of the infantry. The Continentals carried a mixture of firelocks. Some troops still used muskets that had been produced in the various states, most of which were patterned roughly after the standard British weapon. There were also captured British arms and imports from the Netherlands and other European sources. Daniel Morgan's soldiers carried rifles. Washington was anxious to standardize infantry weapons, however, and he wanted his regiments to be equipped with the newer French muskets whenever possible.

Brig. Gen. Henry Knox fostered a growing competence in the Continental artillery. A Boston bookseller, Knox had read widely on military matters, and, as a self-taught artillerist, he famously had orchestrated the delivery of cannons from Fort Ticonderoga, New York, and other northern posts to Washington's army at Cambridge, Massachusetts, in January 1776. After the British evacuated Boston, Knox rose steadily through the army's ranks to become the chief of Continental artillery and was one of the commander in chief's most trusted lieutenants.

At Valley Forge, Knox established armories and repair shops for his guns, and he carefully supervised the training of his gunners. He also reorganized and reequipped the artillery arm, making good use of imported French guns and pieces captured at Saratoga. Knox had four battalions, cobbled together from units that had been raised originally as various state artillery companies. The latter usually had two 3-, 4-, or 6-pounder artillery pieces each. The battalions did not receive formal numeric designations until 1779; before then, the army knew them only by the names of their colonels. The future 1st Continental Artillery Regiment was [Col. Charles] Harrison's Continental Artillery Regiment; the 2d was [Col. John] Lamb's; the

Henry Knox, Charles Willson Peale, undated (*Library of Congress*)

3d was [Col. John] Crane's; and the 4th was [Col. Thomas] Procter's. These units never deployed as full battalions; their various companies went to different theaters. At Monmouth Courthouse, however, each battalion would be represented by at least one company. By the late spring of 1778, their training was well advanced and the artillerists' esprit de corps was among the highest in the army. Three of the battalions even had their own bands.

By spring 1778, the Continental Line was mending. The rebuilt regiments were still too thin, and Washington wanted to consolidate the many weaker units into fewer but stronger regiments—a task far from completed by the end of the Valley Forge encampment. Even so, the troops functioned in the face of impediments few European forces could tolerate. Continentals made do with less of everything and got more out of what they had. The troops were increasingly effective in maintaining weapons and equipment; specialists in various departments could bake bread, sew clothes, and fabricate gun and vehicle parts. The soldiers were never self-sufficient, but they learned to do a great deal to help themselves. Problems remained. Washington was never fully happy with any area of army administration, and he was under no illusion his regiments would emerge from Valley Forge as the equals of the best British units. Rebel cavalry remained a problem: many riders were of high quality, but Washington never had enough of them because mounts were expensive to obtain and to maintain. The army had to rely heavily on European officers for military engineering. Medical services seldom functioned well and frequently were the source of turmoil among feuding personnel. Yet, by late spring 1778, the general considered the Continental Line a substantially improved force; he finally had a version of the "respectable army" he had wanted for so long.

The improving circumstances of the army lifted morale to its highest level in months—and morale soared higher still when the troops learned America no longer was fighting alone. In February 1778, the French recognized American independence and joined the new republic in a military alliance. War between France and Britain soon followed. The colonial rebellion would morph into a world war, with Spain entering on the side of the French in 1779, and the Dutch following suit in 1780. It was a disaster for Britain, which would fight largely alone, although it did have treaties with several German states that were supplying troops. News of the Franco-American alliance reached Valley Forge on 3 May, and Washington greeted it in terms of divine intervention. "The Almighty ruler of the Universe," he told the army, had favored America by "raising us up a powerful Friend among the Princes of the Earth to establish our liberty and Independence." The general proclaimed a day of thanksgiving with a parade in honor of the alliance, cheers for Louis XVI, artillery salutes, and (perhaps best of all for the rank and file) a special issue of rum.

Thus, as the spring of 1778 neared its end, Washington commanded a much-improved army. How much better, however, and how it would do against British veterans remained to be seen, especially in the new context of an international war and a changing strategic landscape. For Washington and his lieutenants, the chief concern was no longer the rebuilding of the Continental Line; rather, they needed to decide what to do with the revitalized army. In a series of councils of war during the spring, the rebel generals remained conservative. They advised Washington to stand on the defensive at Valley Forge while the army recovered its strength. They would react to enemy developments and would fight if attacked, but they would forego the initiative. Washington agreed, seeing no real alternative. With the coming of a new campaign season, however, that thinking would have to change.

Britain's Strategic Shift

Washington was not alone in pondering the future. In fact, the British were well ahead of him in that regard. After Burgoyne's surrender at Saratoga and Howe's failure to destroy the Continentals, Prime Minister Frederick, Lord North's government concluded that a military decision in the northern colonies was unlikely. This realization, compounded by war with France, compelled a radical change in imperial strategy—a change based on cold-blooded realism. New operations in the American North seemed a waste of precious personnel, materiel, and money. Moreover, the French were in a position to threaten Britain's lucrative sugar-producing Caribbean colonies—the loss of which would have been fiscally disastrous for the empire. The British had to keep a wary eye on the Spanish, too. Britain could not fight everywhere, and the government concluded that it had to make better use of its military and financial resources. That meant a redeployment away from the North. The Crown would continue to hold New York City and its environs, but Britain would redeploy most of its military assets to regions of greater military promise and of higher strategic and financial value.

However, the new British strategy implied no intention to settle for less than complete victory over the rebels. British plans for 1778 were ambitious. As an initial step, Germain finally accepted William Howe's resignation, and the frustrated general sailed for home on 24 May. In his place, Germain appointed Lt. Gen. Sir Henry Clinton. It was a logical choice. Clinton knew America well. His father had been the colonial governor of New York, and young Henry had held a militia commission; as a redcoat, he had compiled a solid service record during the Seven Years' War. Clinton had come back to America in 1775 with Howe and Burgoyne, the three generals the Crown considered best suited to deal with the rebellion. He had served under Howe, and in 1776, he was instrumental in securing the British victory on Long Island, New York. While Howe had moved against Philadelphia in 1777, Clinton had remained in New York where he tried (unsuccessfully) to relieve patriot pressure on Burgoyne's ill-fated army. Critical of Howe's leadership—he never thought the Philadelphia invasion was a good idea—Clinton now would have to make the best of the uncertain British situation in America.

The new British commander hated his orders. The plans called for the redeployment of many of Clinton's soldiers in a new effort in the American South—where the ministry hoped for significant loyalist support—and to bolster garrisons in Florida and the valuable Caribbean sugar islands. The ministry also would keep a worried eye on Europe, which meant that Clinton could expect no significant reinforcements. His orders allowed him to keep Philadelphia if he considered it possible, but Clinton knew he lacked the troops to stay in Pennsylvania. The orders staggered British morale. The city had been the only prize in 1777, and the army had bled and fought hard to take it. Much of the British officer corps was furious. Loyalists, many of whom had reason to fear their fate at the hands of vengeful patriots after a British exit, were appalled. But orders were orders:

Clinton was to return his army to New York for redeployment. He immediately began planning their departure, and—unknowingly—he set the stage for the dramatic final chapter of the Philadelphia Campaign, a chapter that became a campaign unto itself.

OPERATIONS

Moving an army, much less evacuating a major city, is a difficult operation to hide, and this was certainly the case for the British in late May and early June 1778. No matter how carefully the British tried to mask their intensions, word began to filter out of Philadelphia that something significant was imminent. Indeed, Washington had a well-informed intelligence operation running in and around the city, and as early as 14 May (or very soon thereafter), the rebels learned that the British had begun packing their heavy equipment. It was increasingly obvious that the enemy was going to decamp. But when and how? Washington needed to find out, and on 18 May he dispatched an intelligence mission toward Philadelphia. It was a venture that barely avoided costing him a significant part of his army—and its youngest major general.

Lafayette Rushes In

Washington assigned the mission to 20-year-old Maj. Gen. Marie-Joseph Paul Yves Roch Gilbert du Motier, Marquis de Lafayette—the scion, as his long name denoted, of a noble French family of considerable lineage and wealth. Only a junior officer in France, and without an active command, Lafayette formed an idealistic

Marie-Joseph Paul Yves Gilbert du Motier, Marquis de La Fayette, Joseph-Désiré Court, 1834 (*Wikimedia Commons*)

view of the patriot cause as noble and just. Seeking military glory, he sailed for America at his own expense—and against the wishes of his family and the French court—to volunteer his services to the Continental Army. In commissioning the marquis a major general, Congress had intended to give him a courtesy appointment, hoping the well-connected young marquis might help garner tangible French support for the revolution. No one expected the then 19-year-old to receive an actual command, but Lafayette badly wanted a combat assignment. He had been at the Battle of Brandywine (during which he was hit in the leg), but not as a unit leader. His first command in actual combat came in November 1777 when, under Nathanael Greene, he had led a detachment of Continental riflemen and members of the New Jersey militia in a forty-five-minute skirmish against a Hessian picket at Gloucester, New Jersey. He had done well in this engagement, and it prompted Washington, who had come to befriend the young man, to recommend him for division command. Lafayette had soldiered faithfully in the Mohawk Valley in New York and at Valley Forge, but he was untried in any significant combat role.

Washington had gambled on a maturity in the Frenchman that would prove problematic. The marquis would have roughly 2,100 troops, including attached personnel from the Pennsylvania militia, and five artillery pieces. He also had specific orders. Lafayette was to advance as close to British lines as he safely could; he would then provide security for Valley Forge and the neighboring region, intercept enemy communications and patrols, and report on any information about British movements and "designs." It was these enemy designs that Washington cared most about. Lafayette was to use "trusty and intelligent spies" and, one assumes, whatever means possible to discover any British preparations "to evacuate Philadelphia. This is a point," the commander in chief stressed, "which it is of the utmost importance to ascertain."

He also wanted to know where the British were going. Lafayette had permission to attack any withdrawing enemy units, but he was to avoid unnecessary risks. "You will remember that your detachment is a very valuable one, and that any accident happening to it would be a severe blow to this army," Washington added. He warned Lafayette to keep moving, as any fixed position would pose a tempting target. Later on 18 May, the enthusiastic major general led his detachment out of camp—and into harm's way.

Crossing the Schuylkill River at Swede's Ford, Lafayette marched about half the distance (around 12 miles) to Philadelphia, taking position on Barren Hill, a prominent piece of terrain rising from the riverbank. The high ground was relatively close to Swede's and Matson's Fords over the Schuylkill and commanded the key road network leading from Philadelphia toward Whitemarsh and Valley Forge. Lafayette posted a brigade, under Brig. Gen. Enoch Poor, with the five guns on Barren Hill, and he stationed 600 soldiers from the Pennsylvania militia, under Brig. Gen. James Potter, on his left, toward Whitemarsh. A party of allied Oneida Indians and some fifty Continentals under Capt. Allen McLane patrolled to the south. Lafayette may have set about his intelligence-gathering mission, although activities in that regard are hazy and there is little evidence he learned anything of value. Whether he intended to move from Barren Hill is also unknown, but, in stationing Poor's brigade there even temporarily, he had ignored Washington's warning to remain mobile.

Lafayette should have known that a stationary concentration of rebel troops might attract the attention of even the inert William Howe. In fact, the marquis must have known that only three weeks before, a sizable patriot command actually had. On 1 May, at the Battle of Crooked Billet, which had taken place only 13 miles from Barren Hill, the British had surprised and routed an incautious encampment of 300 to 500 Pennsylvania militia members, many of whom were asleep. What happened at Crooked Billet should have taught Lafayette to keep his troops on the move, but instead, as the commander in chief had feared, Lafayette became a target.

In Philadelphia, the British learned of Lafayette's position at Barren Hill on 19 May, probably from a loyalist spy. Clinton had joined the soon-to-depart Howe the previous day, and the generals had spent their hours in celebration as Howe's officers fêted him with an extravagant send-off party. When Howe realized that the rebels had forwarded a significant force, now seemingly in a fixed and vulnerable position, he came alive. He would go after Lafayette in overwhelming strength, and it would be a chance to end his disappointing American command with a victory.

While Howe was organizing his strike, Washington clearly was concerned about the marquis and, perhaps, the decision to assign the mission to the Frenchman. Even as Lafayette marched, Washington decided the young general would need support. Then, as reports reached Valley Forge of sudden British activity, the commanding general's closest aides became concerned for the marquis's safety. They communicated urgently with other Continental officers, directing them to send detachments to assist Lafayette. Events, however, moved too quickly for any reinforcements to reach him. Lafayette was on his own.

Howe's plan to catch the Frenchman was a good one. Late on 19 May, he moved his troops north from Philadelphia in three columns. Howe and Clinton accompanied a column intending to block any effort Lafayette made to escape southward. Some 2,000 troops followed Maj. Gen. Charles Grey through Germantown, Pennsylvania, to block the rebel left. The largest British column, around 5,000 redcoats under Maj. Gen. James Grant, marched toward the north of Barren Hill, aiming to cut off Lafayette from Swede's and Matson's Fords. If everything went as planned, the British would catch Lafayette by surprise, cut off all escape routes, and pin the encircled rebels against the Schuylkill. Lafayette would have faced the brutal choice of surrendering or fighting a disastrous, losing battle.

It did not come to that. Two of the British columns, those under Howe and Clinton and those under Grey, moved into position as intended, but Grant, for reasons never fully explained, was late. His delay saved Lafayette, although barely. As the British approached early on 20 May, the militia fled, leaving Lafayette's left wide open. Fortunately, rebel scouts alerted him to the developing threat. To his credit, he reacted promptly, ordering a withdrawal north toward Matson's Ford. He avoided Grant by taking a track unknown to the British, leaving some of his trailing elements to skirmish with Grant's troops. The Oneidas did much of this rearguard fighting, initially stopping some British horses with scattered musketry and arrows. (*See Map 2.*) Then, pressed hard by advancing redcoat infantry, the Oneidas fell back, fighting, and crossed the Schuylkill to safety at Matson's Ford, where they joined Lafayette's main body. Lafayette had conducted a disciplined march that took him steadily out of trouble, and he led his detachment safely back to Valley Forge.

Casualties apparently were limited to several soldiers who drowned while fording the Schuylkill. It had been a close call.

Reactions to the Barren Hill affair—it was never a battle—varied. The incident had denied Howe a redemptive final bow, and there were recriminations. Among the British officer corps, there were murmurs accusing Grant of inexcusable lethargy and blaming him for Lafayette's escape. Royal artilleryman Lt. Col. Francis Downman, a fine soldier with a flair for sarcasm, was furious. "D—— your buts," he fumed. Grant had been inexcusably slow and had ruined an encirclement plan that should have succeeded. "Now, sir, you can see why I d——d the buts. General Grant . . . ought to have advanced with all his speed. How fortunate is our most gracious sovereign to be blessed with such truly intrepid soldiers, and such consummate generals. D—— the buts, I wish he were drowned in a butt of Yankee cider."

The patriots also knew that Lafayette narrowly had escaped a fiasco, but they put a positive spin on the affair. In Washington's telling, a clever young major general had foxed the arrogant British. The flight of the militia, the general told New York delegate Gouverneur Morris, had "very near" found the marquis "in a snare—in fact he was in it—but by his *own dexterity*, or the Enemy's *want of it*, he disengaged himself in a very soldierlike manner & by an orderly, and well conducted retreat got out" of trouble with minimal losses. The Frenchman "came handsomely off, & the Enemy returned disappointed & disgraced." Despite his upbeat demeanor, Washington must have realized that the near-disaster at Barren Hill reflected poorly on his own judgment. He had put a significant operation into the hands of a 20-year-old, and it would not be the last time.

Whatever his thoughts on Barren Hill, Washington did not dwell on them. He had more important matters to consider. What, for instance, was Sir Henry Clinton going to do, and what could the patriot army do about it? These were the same questions Washington had posed in his letter to Landon Carter, and he was genuinely perplexed. He was sure that the British had to choose between continuing to fight in the North American colonies or

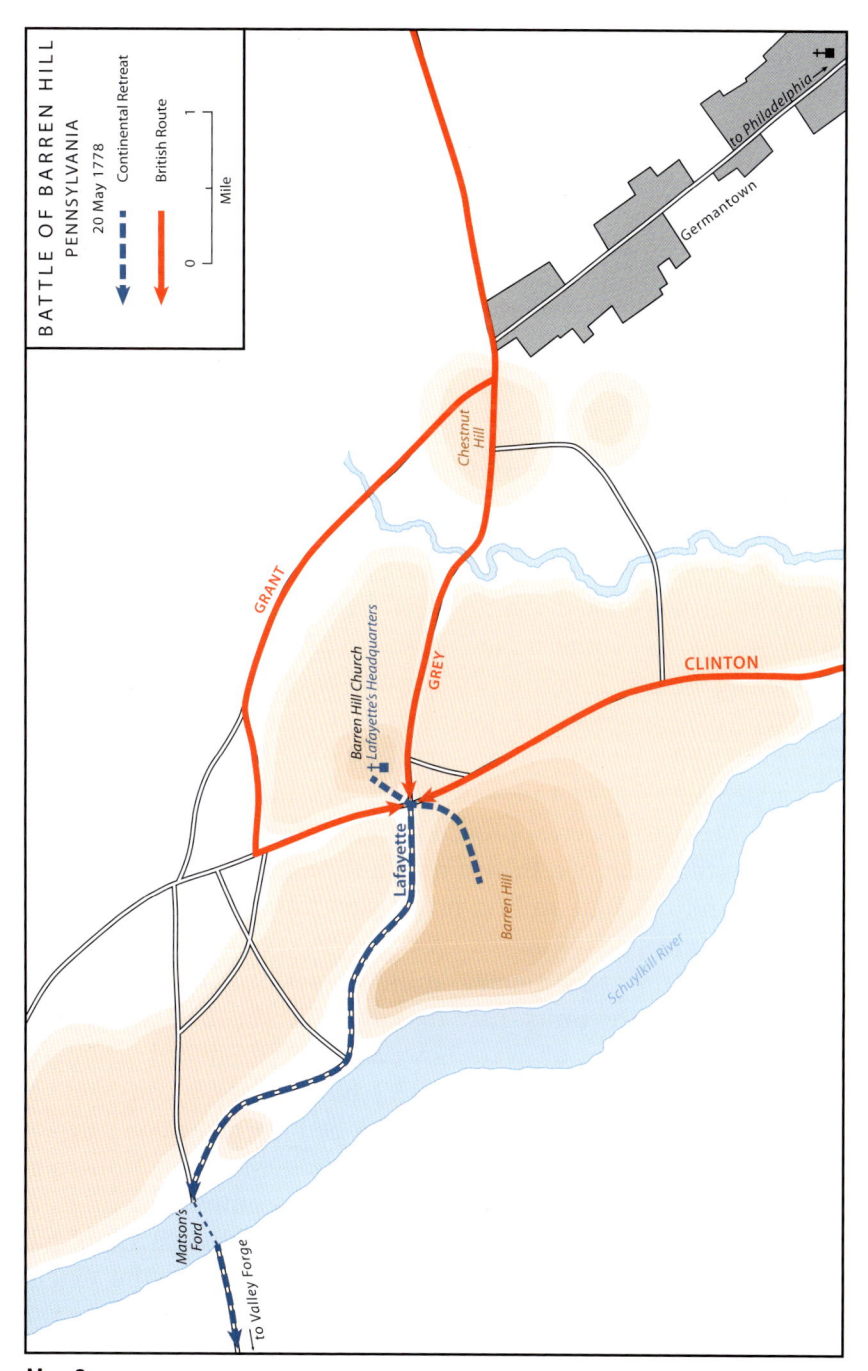

Map 2

redeploying to defend their Caribbean islands, and he was equally sure they would "march the flower of their Army, unincumbered with Baggage, through the Jerseys" in order to get back to New York. He was unsure whether he could stop them. His generals continued to counsel caution, and he worried that if he moved too early—presumably into New Jersey—in anticipation of the British march, Clinton might send a party against Valley Forge, which then would be lightly defended and which still held 1,000 sick personnel and stocks of vital supplies. Washington felt his hands were tied until British plans became clear.

Preparations for Philadelphia

Although Washington could only guess at British intentions, he did take some precautionary steps. As early as mid-March, the general had dispatched the 2d New Jersey Regiment, under Col. Israel Shreve, to southern New Jersey to assist the local militia in countering British foraging. In early May, he sent Col. Matthias Ogden's 1st New Jersey Regiment to join Shreve when increasing loyalist activity became a concern. Shortly after Barren Hill, he dispatched the rest of the New Jersey Brigade (under Brig. Gen. William Maxwell), then approaching 900 strong, to join Shreve and Ogden. In the event of a British march through the state, he hoped Maxwell and the state militia might slow Clinton enough for the Continentals to catch him.

In 1776, the New Jersey militia's performance had been problematic; entire units had dissolved in the face of Howe's invasion. Two years of war, however, had produced dramatic changes. Much of the citizen-soldiery now had seen considerable duty, including combat, and the British had learned to be wary of them. Militia leadership had improved as well. Maj. Gen. Philemon Dickinson had emerged as a capable militia commander, and he worked easily with Maxwell to coordinate skirmishing actions and trade intelligence. Washington trusted Dickinson to the extent that he sometimes forwarded orders to Maxwell through the militia general.

Philemon Dickinson, etching by Albert Rosenthal after Benson Lossing, 1863 (Emmet Collection, New York Public Library)

    In fact, Continentals and citizen-soldiers were effectively collaborating in joint operations, fighting "in concert" in what today would be termed compound or combined warfare. Not all New Jersey militia members were reliable partners with the patriot regulars, but, by the late spring of 1778 enough of them were, and it would be difficult to imagine a large unit of the New Jersey militia dispersing in a fashion similar to the Pennsylvania militia's flight at Barren Hill. Sir Henry Clinton would have his hands full in "the Jersies."

Sir Henry Clinton, John Smart, 1777 (National Institute of American History and Democracy)

    Washington may not have had a precise idea where he might confront Clinton, but the rebel general made some educated guesses. He had campaigned extensively in New Jersey, and he had some idea of how Clinton might try to march across the state.

    He knew the routes the Continentals would have to follow in order to catch him. Any chase, however, would require careful logistics planning, so Washington set Greene and Wadsworth to work. New Jersey became a hive of activity as commissary personnel scoured the countryside for food and forage, and Greene pressed quartermaster officers to move wagons and teams to Coryell's Ferry (present-day Lambertville) on the New Jersey side of the Delaware River, the likely crossing point when and if the army moved from Valley Forge. Greene also tried to divine where Clinton might head, and he guessed it might be Perth Amboy, New Jersey, from which the redcoats easily could get back to New York. Accordingly, the quartermaster general ordered food, forage, and supplies cached every 15 miles or so north of Clinton's possible line of march. Greene never felt that he had enough transport or that deliveries of supplies were moving fast enough, but if Washington chose to campaign in New Jersey, he would have what he needed. Ever since their near collapse in the early winter, rebel logistics were now functioning at a high level.

It was impossible to hide all of this activity. Clinton knew the patriots were anticipating a British march through New Jersey and knew he might have to fight his way to New York. War-wise civilians sensed that something big was in the offing. By late May, many of them, especially in the areas opposite Philadelphia, were taking precautions, driving livestock to hidden locations in the woods and concealing family valuables. New Jersey, already the scene of so much fighting—by 1783, the state would see more combat than any other state—was tensing for more.

Washington was prudent in his concerns for the security of Valley Forge, but he need not have worried. Clinton had no intention of striking north; he had more than enough to do in planning the evacuation of Philadelphia and preparing for a new campaign. He knew it would not be easy. The *Royal Navy* announced that it lacked the shipping to transport the army, camp followers, fleeing loyalists, animals, and equipment to New York. Sir Henry therefore assigned the sick and wounded, military dependents, loyalist civilians, and some Hessian regiments to the available ships. The rest of his army—some 20,800 soldiers and camp followers—would have to walk across New Jersey.

Preparations commenced shortly before Howe's 24 May departure. The British had begun packing heavy equipment in mid-May, and on 30 May Clinton sent two regiments to Cooper's Ferry (modern Camden), New Jersey, the army's primary rendezvous across the Delaware. On 3 June, the British started moving wagons and provisions across the river; more baggage and the first troops crossed on the 15th. Meanwhile, troops in Philadelphia began destroying unserviceable equipment and anything else they were not taking with them. On 18 June, Clinton's entire army had made it across the Delaware and was consolidating in a huge temporary encampment stretching from Cooper's Ferry east, almost 5 miles, to Haddonfield, New Jersey. There was also a small garrison on the banks of the Delaware at Billingsport, New Jersey, and these troops soon marched to Haddonfield. Also on 18 June, the *Royal Navy* sailed with its share of the evacuation. All of this was an impressive logistical feat, the work of a competent, professional military, and it had happened without the slightest interruption by the rebels. The Philadelphia occupation was over.

The March through New Jersey

With headquarters in Haddonfield, Clinton took stock. He knew where he was going. In May, he had sent an engineer officer, John Hills, on reconnaissance into New Jersey. Somehow, Hills and his small escort had avoided detection and returned to provide Clinton with detailed notes and maps. So informed, the general planned a 90-mile trek to New York, a bit more or less depending upon the route pursued. The first half of the march would be within what is known today as New Jersey's Inner Coastal Plain, a region of fertile terrain interspersed with gentle hills, streams, wetlands, and cedar and pine forests. The plain spanned the state between the Delaware River and Raritan Bay in the east. The roads were sometimes poor, but they were part of an established corridor connecting Philadelphia and New York, and the main roads were generally passable. The army was prepared for road maintenance—it even had bridging equipment—and it would not be cutting its way through a wilderness. Initially, Clinton would head northeast, toward Allentown in central New Jersey, about 40 miles distant. At Allentown, Clinton would have to decide on the final leg of his journey. By 18 and 19 June, amid occasional rebel sniping, the entire army was in motion.

As he had with the evacuation, Clinton had thoroughly planned the march. Coordinating the movement of some 20,800 people, 46 artillery pieces and ammunition stores, perhaps 5,000 horses, and 1,500 horse-drawn wagons and carts was no easy matter. Security and efficiency mandated strict "discipline and good order." Clinton's orders were fairly standard for an eighteenth-century army on the move, but he wanted the rules understood from the beginning. Officers were to keep a tight rein on their units; looting and "straggling" risked summary execution. Civilians with the army were to register their professions, former addresses, and who had recommended them for the march. Clinton allowed two women per company to draw rations, and women were to march with the baggage of their corps. The provost marshal was "to drum out any woman who dare[d] to disobey this order."

The British army marched in two roughly equal divisions (*Map 3*). One was under the command of Lt. Gen. Charles, 2nd Earl Cornwallis. Aristocratic, aggressive, and talented, the earl was a veteran of the 1776 and 1777 campaigns under Howe, and he had returned from leave in Britain shortly before the evacuation of the city. He was now Clinton's second-in-command. Clinton accompanied *Cornwallis's Division*, which comprised about 10,470 individuals, including 10,020 combatants and roughly half of the army's artillery. There also were 448 or so noncombatants, including 355 women. The division held the elite of the British army. Among other units were two battalions of the *Brigade of Foot Guards*; the *1st* and *2d Grenadier Battalions*; the *1st Light Infantry Battalion*; the *Royal Highland Regiment* or the *42d Foot*, also known informally as the *Black Watch*; the experienced *33d Foot* (Cornwallis held the ceremonial title of colonel of the *33d*); and the loyalist *Queen's American Rangers*, one of the best combined arms units—light horse and light infantry—of the war, led by the enterprising Lt. Col. John Graves Simcoe. These were certainly among the best troops all of Europe could field.

On the trek to Allentown, whenever possible, Cornwallis's combat-heavy division took roads to the north of the rest of the army, anticipating that any enemy threats probably would come from that

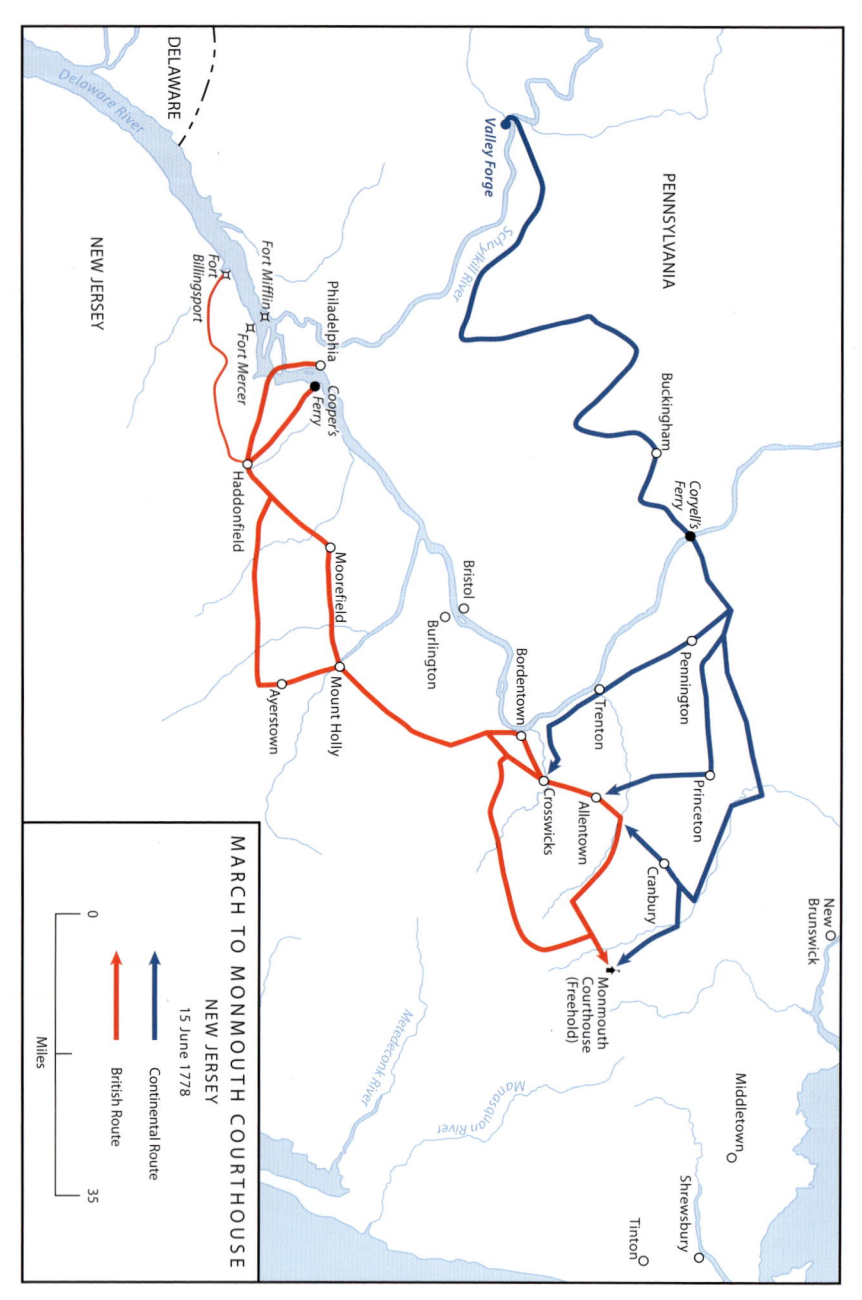

Map 3

direction. Brig. Gen. Alexander Leslie commanded the division vanguard, composed of the *7th (Royal Fusiliers) Foot, 26th Foot*, and *63d Foot*. Leslie would move against targets of opportunity, including rebel forces of any size approaching the Cornwallis-Clinton column. Regular flanking parties would see to rebel skirmishers, which appeared in growing numbers as the British pushed inland.

The second division marched under Lt. Gen. Wilhelm Reichsfreiherr von Innhausen und Knyphausen, an accomplished German commander. As a junior officer, he had fought gallantly during the Seven Years' War, ending the conflict as a lieutenant colonel. By 1775, Knyphausen was a lieutenant general under Frederick the Great—the rank and post Franklin had credited to Steuben—and the following year, he shipped out to America as the second-in-command of the Hessians in British employ. He became their commander in 1777. Knyphausen fought effectively at the Battles of White Plains and Fort Washington in 1776 and in the Philadelphia Campaign in 1777. Clinton thought highly of him, and he would retain that respect on the march.

Knyphausen's Division generally used roads parallel to and south of Cornwallis and Clinton. The Hessian general had about 9,150 men and women in his column, as well as 3 children. Some 7,696 were combatants, including all the loyalist units except the *Queen's American Rangers*. While the rangers were excellent troops, most of the Tory units had received only rudimentary training and had seen little (if any) serious combat. They lacked the skills of the redcoats and Germans; the march would be a learning experience. Among the noncombatants were the support units: paymaster, quartermaster, engineer, medical, bridgemaster, and other specialized personnel. Knyphausen also had James Grant, still under a shadow after Barren Hill, who commanded two brigades—nine regiments, including the *4th (King's Own) Foot* and the *23d (Royal Welch Fusiliers) Foot*. Numbers are not exact, as various units moved between divisions over the course of the march. Each division carried its share of wagons to support immediate needs, but Knyphausen had the heavy baggage train, including provisions and stores. The German took the train's security seriously—it was also a constant worry of Clinton's—

because there was little room for error. With its numerous wagons and carts, the train at times extended almost 12 miles. It was a tempting target, and rebels constantly probed for weak points in the security screen. In fact, both divisions moved in a state of high alert, with flanking skirmishers and mounted patrols constantly on the move.

Clinton was in no hurry. His soldiers plodded through "excessive heat"—the temperature was generally above 90 degrees and sometimes well above—torrential rains, and swarming mosquitoes. Daily treks began early, taking advantage of lower morning temperatures; the divisions rested in the hotter afternoons. Rebel detachments hovered on their flanks destroying bridges and felling trees across roads, although such tactics occasioned only minimal delays. The British expected such annoyances and dealt with them routinely. They also skirmished with the militia and Maxwell's New Jersey Brigade, although the clashes were small, and casualties on both sides were minimal. The fighting did not reach the main columns. All of these factors explained some of Clinton's lethargic pace—the army averaged only some 10 miles per day—but hardly all of it. The chief factor was Clinton's hope for an engagement with Washington. As much as the British commander resented his orders to retreat, he planned to make the best of his trek, hoping his very deliberate march would allow the rebel army to catch up. With any luck, he would find a way to draw Washington, or at least a major part of the Continental Army, into a real fight, if not a decisive showdown.

Washington operated cautiously as the British crossed into New Jersey. Throughout the spring, his officers had agreed to react to enemy initiatives rather than boldly attacking. Yet, on 17 June, a new council of war was a bit more contentious. Seventeen officers attended or gave written opinions; all but two men advised against any dramatic response to Clinton's evacuation. In particular, Major Generals Charles Lee and Steuben still doubted the Continentals could handle the British regulars. Again, caution prevailed.

Lee's presence at the council was notable. A former British officer with considerable experience in America and Europe during and after the Seven Years' War, he had settled in Virginia in 1774.

Charles Lee, Esq'r., Major General of the American Forces, etching, artist unknown, 1780 (*Library of Congress*)

Lee was an early advocate of independence, and Congress commissioned him a major general, ranking him behind only Washington and Artemas Ward of Massachusetts. Upon Ward's resignation, Lee became second-in-command. He served capably in various commands, but, in late 1776, he became indiscreetly critical of Washington after patriot defeats around New York. In December, Lee's capture by a British patrol in New Jersey probably saved the patriots from an open split between the army's two senior generals. Finally exchanged, Lee returned to duty on 21 May 1778—that is, less than a month before the British left Philadelphia. The man had a temper and was prone to sarcasm, which made him few friends, and after returning to Valley Forge, he objected to Steuben's training regimen and to Washington's insistence on forging a regular army. Lee largely preferred militia operations and guerrilla warfare. In this, Lee was out of step with the commander in chief and most of the officer corps. Moreover, he was friendly with the likes of Mifflin and Gates, leaders in the Conway Cabal that had challenged Washington's leadership over the winter. With potential operations looming, Washington had let this pass and welcomed Lee back, but the men were not close. Other officers, notably Greene, who had seen the army change at Valley Forge, were leery of Lee. These doubts about Lee would have a significant impact on the ensuing campaign.

Other officers at the council, including Greene, Lafayette, and Anthony Wayne, differed with Lee's cautionary opinion and argued for bringing Clinton at least to battle, if not to a general engagement. Wayne, a veteran Pennsylvanian, had served in Canada, upper New York, and, after being promoted to brigadier general in February 1777, with Washington's main army. The British had routed his command at the Battle of Paoli on 20 September 1777, but he had fought well at the Battle of Germantown and had served admirably through the Valley Forge winter. Aggressive by nature, Wayne urged no rash measures, but he wanted action. Pennsylvania militia Brig. Gen. John Cadwalader (one of Washington's favorite militia officers) urged an all-out attack. If they lost, so what? The army would recover, and the British, even if they won a battle, could not follow retreating patriots into the New Jersey interior for fear of being "Burgoyned."

Thus, two things were clear: There was still no consensus about how or if to confront Clinton, and now a faction of patriot generals wanted to fight.

Even without a consensus, however, the next day (18 June), events compelled action. Although still without a full appreciation of Clinton's intent, as soon as Washington received confirmation that the British had crossed the Delaware, he dispatched Lee from Valley Forge with the first contingent of Continentals. The following day the rest of the army broke camp, and by the twenty-first, everyone had crossed the river at Coryell's Ferry. Washington then moved south. Unlike Clinton, the patriot general marched through friendly territory. He deployed flanking skirmishers as a standard security measure, but the army endured no enemy harassment and encountered no obstructions on its way over well-established roads. Despite the heat, the Continentals had an easy march.

As the Continental main body moved toward the town of Hopewell, New Jersey, Washington made two detachments. On the twenty-second, he sent Col. Stephen Moylan's dragoons and Col. Daniel Morgan and his riflemen—famous veterans of Saratoga— to link up with Maxwell and Dickinson. He hoped that they could bolster efforts to delay Clinton's march. Then, on the twenty-third, as Washington arrived at Hopewell, he quickly learned that matters southward were heating up.

In fact, 23 June would see more excitement than any other day before the Battle of Monmouth itself. That morning, Leslie's vanguard left the Clinton-Cornwallis camp at Black Horse, New Jersey, pushing north toward Bordentown, New Jersey. His movement was a feint, designed to draw patriot attention away from the village of Crosswicks, New Jersey, about 4 miles up Crosswicks Creek. Clinton intended to transit Crosswicks on the way to Allentown; but the road led through terrain that the British officers thought favored a patriot defense. If Leslie fooled the rebels into thinking the main effort would be through Bordentown, it might mean less trouble at Crosswicks. Skirmishing with the militia began early and intensified as Leslie moved toward a bridge over the creek just outside Bordentown. Rebels on the northern bank mounted a stiff defense, and the fighting went on until dark. After the shooting stopped, Morgan arrived to reinforce the militia. Fighting at the bridge had been noisy but relatively harmless. Dickinson claimed six or seven British killed; but jaeger Lt. Heinrich von Feilitzsch noted only several troops wounded—"God be praised!" Around midnight, shadowed all the way by Morgan, Leslie moved on to Crosswicks, where the rest of the division had arrived. He would find that Cornwallis and Clinton had seen their own share of the day's drama.

Leslie's action at Bordentown had fooled no one. Maxwell informed Washington that Bordentown was simply "a faint," and he readied the New Jersey Brigade to meet Clinton at Crosswicks. With Leslie engaged at Bordentown, Clinton and Cornwallis learned that the rebels were preparing to stand at the Crosswicks bridge, and Clinton sent some dragoons and the *Queen's American Rangers* ahead to seize it. They pushed through the village, but Maxwell held the other side of the bridge with some 500 militia and Continentals. Firing grew heavier as Clinton came up, and the general personally led a ranger company during the attack. This would not be the only time Clinton displayed a dangerous penchant for leading from the front. The weight of British small-arms and artillery fire proved too much for the outnumbered rebels and they fell back, opening the road to Allentown. Clinton called the affair "a trifling skirmish," and, compared to major battles, of course, he was right. Nevertheless, Bordentown and Crosswicks had provided plenty of excitement.

At Hopewell, Dickinson's reports kept Washington fully informed. Indeed, the New Jersey militia general had become well-nigh indispensable. Thus far, Washington had demonstrated a steady hand in coordinating Continental and militia operations, but Dickinson was his chief collaborator. There was no clear chain of command in the forward area, which shifted daily as Clinton moved, but the de facto command fell to Dickinson. He had ordered the stand at Bordentown, sent the militia into action as they moved into areas of active operations, distributed supplies to new arrivals, took charge of enemy prisoners and deserters, and was Washington's best source of intelligence. He ably coordinated operations with Maxwell and other Continental officers and personally roved the British left flank to try to understand what Clinton was doing. When his cousin, Pennsylvania's John Cadwalader, arrived with a small contingent of the Pennsylvania militia, Dickinson arranged for his resupply. It was Dickinson who knew the most about where the various militia and Continental units were, what they were doing, and how to use their resources to the best advantage—that is, he knew how to make compound warfare work. The commander from New Jersey was driving himself hard. On the morning of the twenty-fourth, he apologized to Washington for a nearly illegible dispatch: "your Excellency will excuse this blotted scrawl, as I am rather sleepy."

The flow of intelligence from the south had been steady on the twenty-third, and late that night, Dickinson had forwarded a startling message to Hopewell that Washington received early on 24 June. Based on intelligence gathered over several days, including information from enemy deserters, the militia general concluded that the weather and rebel efforts to impede Clinton's march had had little effect on the British army. Dickinson had rightly interpreted the enemy commander's intentions: Clinton was moving slowly because he was hoping Washington would offer battle. Indeed, the British general was itching "to bring on general action." Now with the enemy's intentions all but certain, how would the Continental commander react?

Passing safely through Crosswicks, Clinton arrived at Allentown on 24 June. *Knyphausen's Division* encamped at nearby Imlaystown, New Jersey. At Allentown, the British had reached a literal crossroad. Two routes lay open to New York. One tracked northeast through New Brunswick, New Jersey, and on to Perth Amboy, where Clinton could cross to British-held Staten Island, New York. A southerly route led through the village of Monmouth Courthouse, New Jersey (also known as Monmouth and Freehold), and on to Sandy Hook, New Jersey, from which the *Royal Navy* could ferry his army to New York. Moving through New Brunswick, Clinton feared, would allow Washington to hit his baggage train as it forded the Raritan River, so he elected the road to Sandy Hook. Clinton also hoped that the terrain toward Monmouth Courthouse would favor him if Washington chose to fight. Thus, on the morning of 25 June, the British left Allentown for Monmouth Courthouse, marching east through intense heat. The rebels were bolder now, dogging the British rear every step of the way. Exhausted, Clinton's troops reached Monmouth Courthouse late on the twenty-sixth.

Instead of moving on the next day, Clinton chose to remain in the village on the twenty-seventh, which proved to be an eventful day. The army could use the rest, and as Clinton was closing on Sandy Hook—only an easy two days' march away—he wanted to give Washington a final chance to offer battle. Clinton deployed the divisions in and around the village in campsites extending roughly 2 miles along the Monmouth Road, with *Knyphausen's Division* on the road east of town. Clinton established his headquarters in a private home in town and was ready to continue his march or to stay and fight.

While happy to have a day of rest, the rank and file were angry. They had endured endless sniping and a constant state of alert. The tension was palpable, and even though the army had retained a reasonable degree of discipline, there had been nasty incidents of plundering and property destruction during the march. Politically motivated, soldiers had lashed out at the homes of prominent rebels. Clinton had strictly prohibited such behavior, but no one ever informed him of which soldiers had been involved. Accumulated resentment broke through on the twenty-seventh. Most officers looked the other way as troops sacked Monmouth Courthouse, pillaging and burning patriot homes and properties. They left Tory civilians alone. Although there had been incidents of violence directed at patriot properties during the march, nothing like the mayhem at Monmouth Courthouse previously had marked the campaign.

When Clinton reached Allentown on 24 June, Washington was in Hopewell, roughly 20 miles to the north. As the rival armies were approaching striking distance, Washington held an important council of war—one of the most important he ever convened until the Yorktown Campaign. It revealed little consensus. Hawks—a minority group that included Greene, Lafayette, and Wayne—argued for hitting Clinton hard without precipitating a general engagement, that is, without committing the entire Continental Army. "If we suffer the enemy to pass through New Jersey without attacking," Greene warned, "I think we shall . . . regret it. . . . People expect something from us and our strength demands it. I am by no means for rash measures," he concluded, "but we must preserve our reputation." It was a political argument aimed at restoring popular faith in Washington and the army after the disappointments of 1777.

Other officers, however, supported Lee's contrary views. Echoing his own comments of 17 June, Lee argued for letting Clinton go, insisting there was no need to risk the army. Would it not be better, he asked, to await French intervention while preserving Continental strength? Lee maintained that a patriot victory in New Jersey would mean little, whereas a serious defeat could do irreversible harm. Lee's ideas had merit. Rebel spirits had soared at news of the French alliance and with the British evacuation of Philadelphia. Clinton also wanted nothing more than to lure Washington into a showdown fight, looking to pounce on any mistake the patriot general made. Lee wanted to avoid just such an eventuality.

Washington chose a middle course. Agreeing to reinforce the troops shadowing Clinton, he dispatched Brig. Gen. Charles Scott with 1,500 "picked men" to support Maxwell's, Morgan's, and Dickinson's militiamen. The picked men were twenty of the most proficient soldiers and a junior officer from each of the army's infantry regiments. It was a temporary formation, roughly analogous to the British light infantry and grenadier battalions formed from the light and grenadier companies of the foot regiments. With these reinforcements, the rebel advance forces now numbered roughly 3,500, and Washington wanted a major general to be in charge of them. When Lee refused the command—he considered it too small—a delighted Lafayette took the assignment. Almost immediately after the council, however, eager hawks, notably Alexander Hamilton, Wayne, and Greene, visited Washington and argued for a still larger reinforcement. One suspects the general was only too happy to take their advice. He sent another 1,000 soldiers south, under Wayne, to join Lafayette. Yet Washington was not rash; he told Lafayette that hitting Clinton was "very desirable," but he warned the Frenchman not to exhaust his troops in the scorching heat. Thus, the Hopewell council had resulted in a considerable movement toward the British. Washington wanted to fight, but he remained cautious as he considered how to do so.

The impetuous Lafayette, however, again ignoring Washington's instructions to avoid unnecessary risks, planned to attack Clinton early on the twenty-sixth. Hastening forward with inadequate supplies and poor intelligence, the Frenchman moved beyond supporting range of Washington's main army. Hamilton, serving as Lafayette's aide, feared a catastrophe. To everyone's relief, Lafayette called off the assault at the last minute, his troops exhausted and his supplies nearly gone. Like the Barren Hill affair, this event was a near brush with calamity, for early on the morning of the twenty-seventh, one of Lafayette's fatigued units—not yet having received the orders to halt—had advanced within a mile of the encampment of the elite British grenadiers before stopping. Again, the marquis had courted disaster, and again, he had gotten away with it.

While Lafayette was closing on the British, Washington was leading the main army south. Apprised of events near Monmouth Courthouse, he ordered Lafayette to Englishtown, New Jersey, 11 miles north. There, the marquis was to meet Lee, who recently had requested the forward command on the basis of its now considerable size. Washington had given Lee the command with the stipulation that Lee support Lafayette if the Frenchman already had engaged. Lafayette, chastened by his brush with disaster, gladly met Lee as ordered.

The opposing armies had reached the eve of battle. As darkness fell on 27 June, Washington's main body was at Manalapan Bridge (sometimes called Penelopen Bridge), about 4 miles northwest of Lee's advance corps of roughly 4,500 at Englishtown. Including the militia, the rebels numbered around 13,000. Clinton had about as many in his division (*Cornwallis's Division*), mostly west of Monmouth Courthouse, and Knyphausen was east of town. The British commander had stayed in town on the twenty-seventh hoping for Washington or one of the patriot generals to pick a fight, and he was about to find he was in luck.

Into Battle at Monmouth Courthouse

Late on the twenty-seventh, Washington met with Lee and his chief subordinates at Englishtown to plan the battle. Everyone later agreed that the commander in chief wanted Lee to advance early on the twenty-eighth and also that Washington issued no specific orders about when, how, or even if to attack. Wayne, who fervently disliked Lee, later admitted that he never heard Washington "give any particular orders for the attack." Indeed, Washington was vague about exactly what he expected, and Lee quite reasonably concluded that his orders were discretionary and that he was to govern his conduct according to events. He told his subordinates exactly that. Lee had Washington's promise, however, that he would support Lee's advance with the main army. But what did that mean? Would Washington commit the main army to combat if Lee engaged? Would he take up a defensive position, perhaps at Englishtown, if Lee needed to fall back? Lee was not sure. These were matters that both Lee and Washington should have clarified. Instead, they were left hanging.

Nor was Lee sure of what other rebel forces were to do on the morning of the twenty-eighth. Dickinson's militia was constantly on the move, although Lee may have been aware that a sizable militia concentration was forming about 2 miles west of Monmouth Courthouse. But could he count on their help in a fight? Daniel Morgan had a significant force of about 800 at Richmond's Mill, New Jersey, south of Monmouth Courthouse and actually behind and to the left of the British; he was in position to hit the enemy in cooperation with Lee. However, in a classic case of the fog of war interceding in events—creating what Prussian military theorist Carl von Clausewitz would come to call "friction," that is, the idea that, in war, easy tasks become more difficult—communication between Morgan, Washington, Greene, and Lee's aides was confusing, which left Morgan unclear as to what he was supposed to do and when he was supposed to do it. Thus, as Lee prepared to move to possible hostile contact, he lacked a full appreciation of the friendly and enemy situations.

Lee moved from Englishtown around 0700, Sunday, 28 June. Earlier, as Washington had directed, Lee had sent Col. William Grayson with a "party of observation" of roughly 700 soldiers toward Monmouth Courthouse to learn what they could of British movements. Lee had a small staff of eight, including senior artillerist Lt. Col. Eleazer Oswald and the French engineer, Brig. Gen. Antoine-Jean-Louis Le Bègue de Presle Duportail, now remembered as the "father" of the Army Corps of Engineers. The rest of the vanguard presented a somewhat confusing order of battle. Six artillery companies were distributed among five brigades or detachments. General Scott's brigade of Virginians initially was commanded by Grayson, because Scott was leading a detachment of picked men, but it is unclear who took over when Grayson assumed command of Lee's advance force. Col. John Durkee commanded [James Mitchell] Varnum's Brigade of Connecticut and Rhode Island regiments (Varnum being absent). Maxwell had the four regiments of the New Jersey Brigade; Scott and Wayne led detachments of picked men, each of which had three or four battalions. Col. Henry Jackson had a detachment of three small "Additional Regiments," which had been raised directly by Congress rather than one of the states and were mostly made up of soldiers from Massachusetts. Finally, Lee had three small troops of mounted militia from New Jersey. The entire vanguard numbered about 4,500. It was a respectable force, but having missed the Valley Forge winter, Lee knew few of his unit commanders well.

Lee's advance was hesitant. Intelligence on the enemy situation was conflicting. Lee learned that Clinton's baggage already was moving—Knyphausen was on the road early—but where was Clinton's main body? About 0730, however, as Lee and Wayne rode forward to reconnoiter and to catch up with Grayson, they heard firing ahead but could not tell who was engaged.

It was not Grayson. The noise came from a sharp clash between the militia and the *Queen's American Rangers*. Led by the intrepid Simcoe, the rangers had come out to chase a rebel scouting party under Steuben. The rangers never caught Steuben's scouts, who got away cleanly. Instead, the loyalists ran into a militia patrol, which they scattered after an intense melee in which Simcoe was wounded.

The rangers then backed off rather than confront another large and strongly posted militia concentration at a prominent hedgerow, a landmark that would figure heavily in the fighting several hours later. Thus, the opening round in the Battle of Monmouth was an all-American affair—the patriot militia *versus* loyalist rangers.

The end of the skirmish, however, revealed nothing of Clinton's dispositions. Lee had moved past the high ground of Perrine Hill to a bridge that spanned the west morass, an area encompassing a swamp and a deeper section of Spotswood Middle Brook. The morass was fordable—around waist-deep—but the key to passage west to Perrine Hill and east toward Monmouth Courthouse was the bridge. Within hours, the short span would figure dramatically in desperate battle, but for the present (about 0745), it marked a halt to Lee's advance. Lee hesitated to push farther, fearing a British attack would catch him in difficult terrain. Militia officers warned of just such a risk. After waiting, and with no solid information about British deployments, an impatient Lee moved, with Wayne in the lead, shortly before 0900.

At this point, Lee was just under 3 miles west of the village. He was moving east, down a relatively open corridor of farms and orchards, although patches of remaining timber would prove dense enough to hide troop concentrations. The terrain was well watered, with boggy ground and small creeks cutting the landscape. A quarter mile east of the west morass was the hedgerow, where the militia had formed earlier. Another half mile east was the so-called middle morass, an agricultural drainage ditch that was, with some difficulty, passable. Another 1½ miles eastward, just north of the village, was the east morass, also a feature of Spotswood Middle Brook. Its deeper northern section was possibly defensible, but it easily could be flanked near the village. To the south was Combs Hill, which offered a sweeping vista of what would prove to be critical sections of the battlefield. All of these terrain features would influence the battle, although Lee hardly could have predicted as much.

Battle began just after 1000. Lee was a bit under a mile northwest of the village and well east of the east morass, when he spotted a redcoat column marching out of Monmouth Courthouse. Lee thought it was a rear guard. He quickly came up with a plan:

Wayne and supporting artillery would stay in position; Wayne was to fix the enemy in place while Lee swung to the left to encircle the redcoats. Lee would bag the lot without risking a major battle, exactly the kind of blow Washington preferred. The scheme was reasonable, and Lee put his troops in motion, executing a competent movement to contact. (*See Map 4.*)

With Lee moving, however, part of Wayne's command exchanged inconsequential long-range fire with the *Queen's American Rangers* and then suddenly came in for a moment of drama. Militia horse units had attracted the attention of the *16th Light Dragoons*, and the rebels cleverly lured them into an ambush. The militia deliberately fled toward Wayne, and the dragoons chased them into the range of one of Wayne's units. A patriot battalion under Col. Richard Butler swung on line—just as Steuben had taught them to do—and fired. The *16th* broke, with several saddles empty.

Butler's rebuff of the *16th* turned out to be the high point of the patriot morning. Lee had run into trouble. The rebels had encountered more than a rear guard. When the rebels appeared, Clinton rode to reconnoiter. Some of his officers had suggested that Washington finally was offering battle, but Clinton thought that the rebels had advanced a smaller force, aiming for his baggage train. In either case, the rebel force was large enough to be an inviting target, and the general felt the terrain favored a counterattack. Could he force the rebels into some of the ravines that intersected the ground west of Monmouth Courthouse and cut them up (just as the militia had warned Lee he might)? Clinton ordered Cornwallis to attack with his entire division. For good measure, he also called on Knyphausen, now well out of town and marching east, to send some Hessian regiments and mounted units. Clinton knew he would not get a general engagement, but the destruction of a significant part of the Continental Army would take some of the sting out of the loss of Philadelphia.

As Cornwallis closed, Lee's plan fell apart. The British bore down on Lee's right, and he realized, while not yet aware of the enemy's real strength, that his plan to envelop a rear guard was now moot. Fearing being flanked on his right, Lee directed Lafayette in that direction, which took the patriots toward the village. Then, as Lee also moved to his right, he was stunned to discover that his left had disappeared. The battalions under Scott and Maxwell had withdrawn. Lacking orders from Lee, the generals had misinterpreted the movements of the other patriot units as a retreat, and they feared being cut off when the British advanced. With his left gone and Cornwallis threatening, Lee was in a quandary. Still east of Monmouth Courthouse, he positioned Lafayette's soldiers (including Wayne) on a quarter-mile front between the oncoming British and the village. Wayne wanted to stay and fight there, but, given the obvious disparity in numbers (Lee now had only 2,500 troops), he knew that pursuing such a battle would be suicidal. At this point, Lee, who was not looking to escape the fight, began looking for a better place to stand.

As Lee pulled back, far to the patriot right—and on the British left—Morgan heard the firing near Monmouth Courthouse. (*See Map 5.*) Wondering what was going on and probably thinking (from the botched communications of the previous night) that no real fighting would occur until the following morning (that is, on Monday, 29 June), he sent a dragoon to locate Lee. The rider found the retreating vanguard, but he encountered Wayne instead of Lee. When the dragoon asked for instructions, Wayne, in all likelihood distracted by the unfolding tactical situation, had none. Nor, inexplicably and inexcusably, did the general send the messenger on to Lee, who never knew Morgan had been trying to get in touch. As a result, Morgan, who was on Clinton's unguarded left, never went into the battle.

In the meantime, Lee and Clinton considered their options. Lee thought he had found promising ground about a mile west of the village. He ordered a concentration near the house of William Kerr, where he hoped to establish a line running north from the house. The French engineer Duportail had suggested the position. The Kerr house was a prominent terrain feature west of Monmouth Courthouse and offered a good view of the town. That view, however, was unsettling. Lee watched as Clinton, in full view of the rebels, stopped briefly in town. Then, deciding the situation looked favorable, he ordered a full-scale assault. Clinton's infantry advanced in two columns, the guards battalions on the right and the grenadiers on the left. The

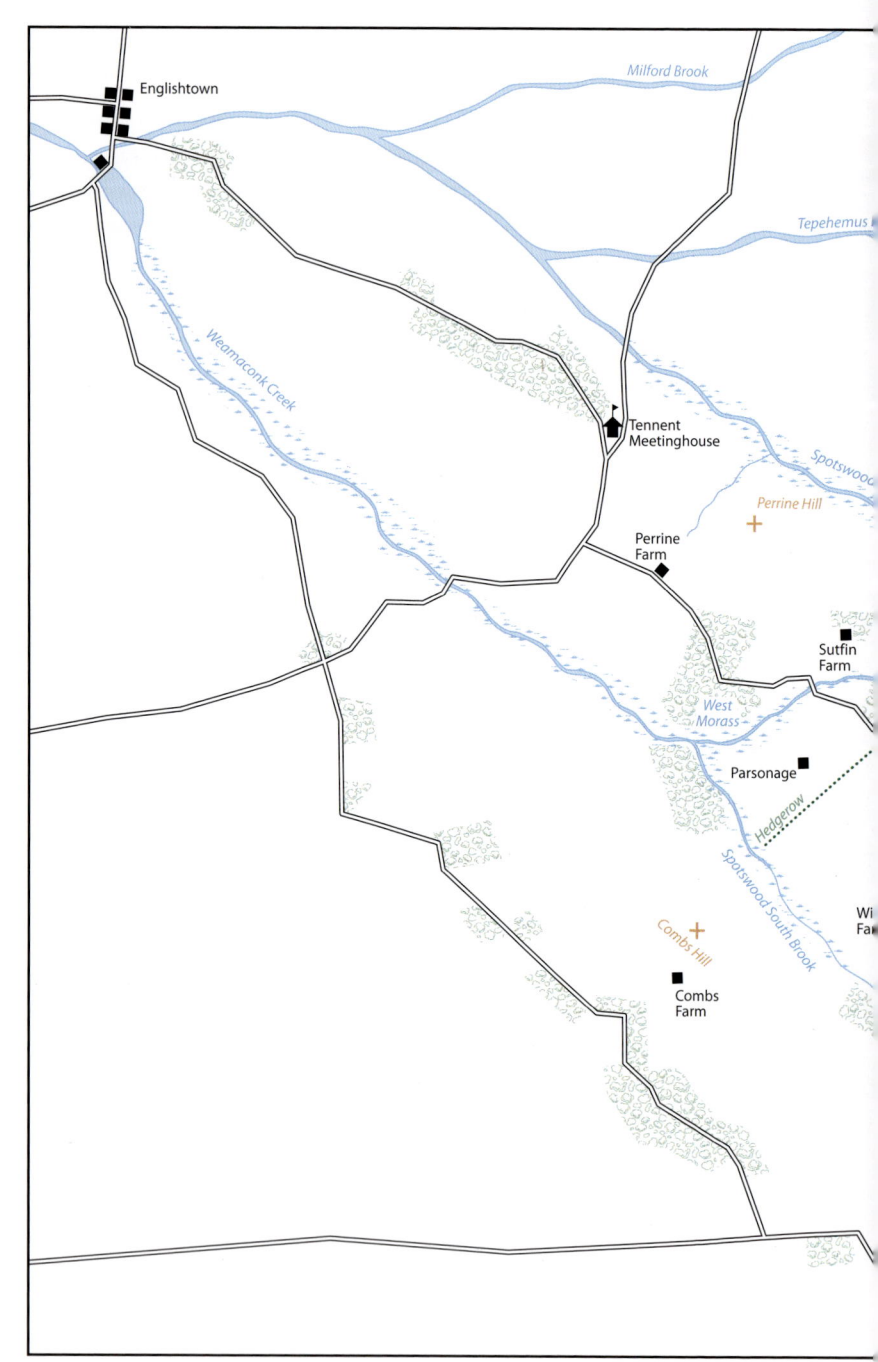

Map 4

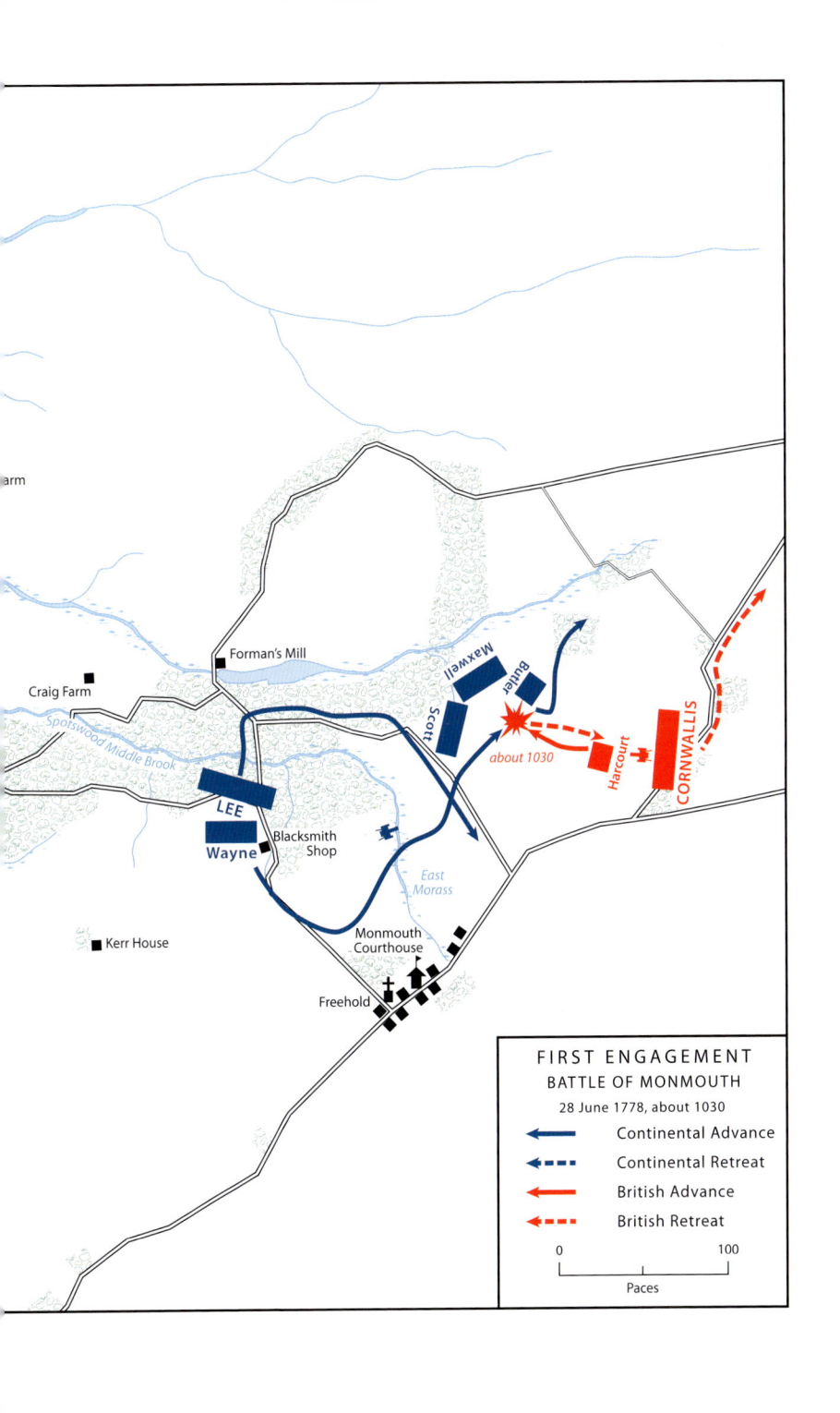

FIRST ENGAGEMENT
BATTLE OF MONMOUTH
28 June 1778, about 1030

⬅ (solid blue)	Continental Advance
⬅ (dashed blue)	Continental Retreat
⬅ (solid red)	British Advance
⬅ (dashed red)	British Retreat

0 — 100
Paces

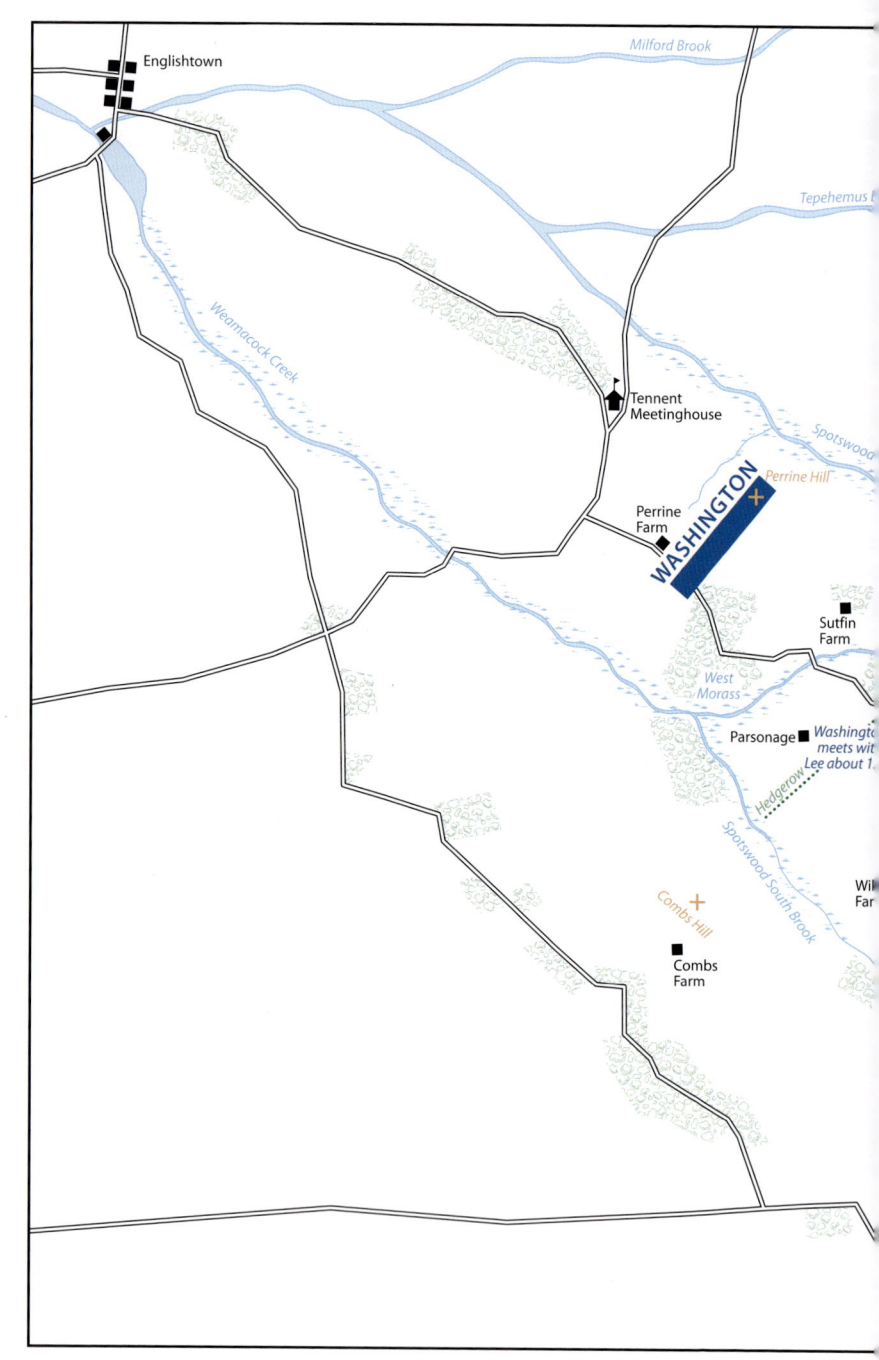

Map 5

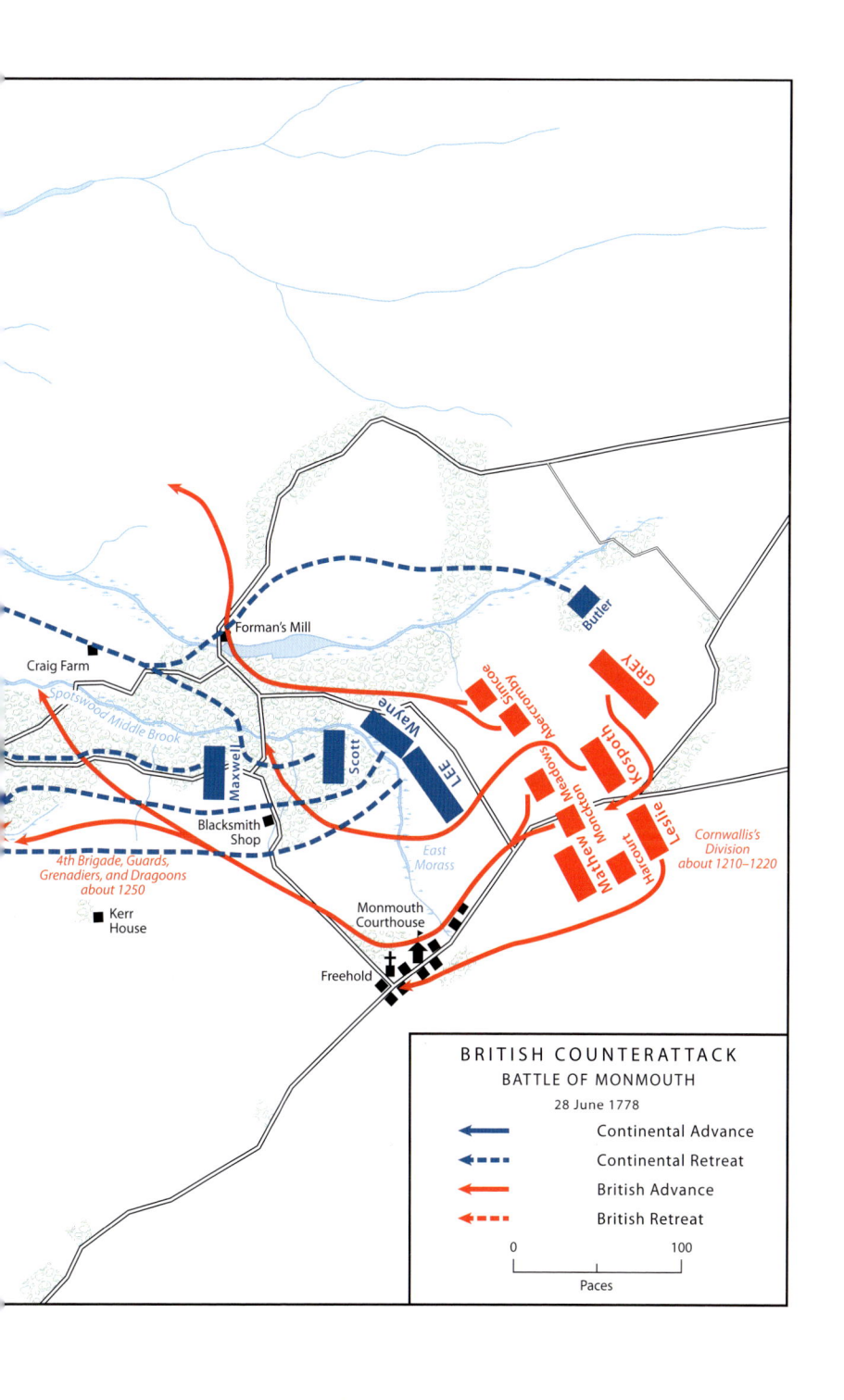

BRITISH COUNTERATTACK
BATTLE OF MONMOUTH
28 June 1778

← Continental Advance
←-- Continental Retreat
← British Advance
←-- British Retreat

0 — 100 Paces

16th Light Dragoons and horse-drawn artillery advanced between the columns. The patriots saw them coming and knew they could not hold the Kerr house line; the numerous British easily could flank them. Wisely, Lee again pulled back, moving west in good order.

Clinton hoped to destroy Lee. The British general knew about the bridge over the west morass, which Lee had crossed earlier. By beating the patriots to that chokepoint, Clinton could trap them on the east side of the morass and bag the lot. He sent Maj. Gen. Charles Grey with his brigade, including the *42d Foot*, on a swing wide to the British right, well to the rebel left. Grey drove his soldiers hard in the brutal heat, wanting to get around the rebels before they knew he was moving. Clinton then sent Brig. Gen. Sir William Erskine with the *1st Light Infantry Battalion* and elements of the *Queen's American Rangers* still farther to the right in another effort to flank the rebels. Initially, the patriot force had no inkling of these enemy movements to their left or that the British commander was throwing virtually everything he had against the Continental vanguard—although it was clear enough that the oncoming British significantly outnumbered Lee's troops.

Lee's continued retrograde remained disciplined, with no panic and little infantry contact. The redcoats came on relentlessly, but the distance between the rivals was too great for effective musketry. Continental artillery, however, covered by militia horse soldiers, maintained a regular fire, which did slow the British advance. The patriots repeatedly limbered up the guns as the redcoats closed, then stopped to resume fire. Movement on both sides was steady, but it was hardly a nip-and-tuck race. The British maintained their lead. After the battle, a few observers complained about disorder in Lee's ranks, but these were instances of units scrambling through ditches or around other terrain features, and officers quickly restored formations. The movement was testimony, in part, to Steuben's work at Valley Forge—the Continentals knew what they were doing.

They were less certain where they were going. After abandoning the line near the Kerr house, Lee was at a loss to find a suitable position. Unexpectedly, an answer presented itself in the form of a local militia officer, Peter Wikoff. He introduced himself to Lee, explained that he knew the ground intimately, and pointed out Perrine Hill (sometimes called Perrine Heights). The terrain was defensible and overlooked the west morass bridge. Lee directed his troops there, with Israel Shreve's 2d New Jersey Regiment, part of Maxwell's New Jersey Brigade, leading the way. With a destination now in view, Lee hastened his tired troops along. He fully intended to fight.

During all of this, Washington was bringing up the main army, as he had promised Lee, but he felt no sense of urgency. In the morning, a few of the Washington's aides had gone forward to contact Lee, but they had reported back to Washington before Lee had begun his retrograde. For all Washington knew, the major general still was trying to make contact with Clinton. At 1130, Washington was having a late breakfast, during which he wrote quick letters to Henry Laurens and Horatio Gates informing them that Lee was moving toward the enemy, and it would be up to Lee to determine how or if to engage. As far as the commander in chief knew, all was well up ahead.

Only when he rode farther toward Monmouth Courthouse did Washington realize that all was *not* well. He saw stragglers trickling to the rear, which raised his apprehension. Then, just south of the Tennent Meetinghouse (one of the most prominent structural features of the battle area), on the approach to Perrine Hill, the general met his aide, Alexander Hamilton. Hamilton informed him of the British advance and warned him of being flanked on the right. Washington quickly ordered Greene to lead a column with supporting artillery down roads to the right to meet any threat—a decision that proved critical later. He next rode to (or very near) the crest of Perrine Hill, where he met Shreve, who had arrived in accordance with Lee's orders. However, the colonel professed not to know the reason for the retreat. Thoroughly alarmed, Washington rode east toward the sound of the guns.

Lee never made it to Perrine Hill. About 1300—probably a bit before—still well on the Monmouth Courthouse side of the bridge and east of the hedgerow, he met Washington. The exhausted major general completely misread the situation. He, quite reasonably, expected a compliment on his skillful retreat, which certainly had saved the vanguard from probable annihilation. Instead, Washington curtly "desire[d] to know," as Lee recalled, "the reason—whence arises this disorder and confusion?" Momentarily lost for words, Lee was "confounded," silenced less by the question than by Washington's tone. The patriot chief, one of Lee's aides remembered, had displayed "considerable warmth." He was unmollified when Lee tried to explain the situation, insisting that Lee should have pushed his attack. Whatever Washington's exact words were, he clearly was annoyed. It made no difference that taking a stand near the village would have been beyond foolhardy; nothing Lee could have said in his defense would have mattered. The bewildered Lee, unsure whether the commander in chief had relieved him, tagged along as Washington rode forward to assess the situation.

The Washington-Lee confrontation became part of American folklore. Over the years, various supposed witnesses to the incident dramatically embellished the story. For example, as old men, Lafayette and Scott gave accounts that had Washington in a perfect fury. The Frenchman remembered the general calling Lee a "damned poltroon," while Scott was astonishingly fanciful. Washington "swore on that day," the old brigadier general insisted, "till the leaves shook on the trees, charming, delightfully. Never did I enjoy such swearing before or since. Sir, on that memorable day, he swore like an angel from Heaven." Neither man, however, had been remotely close enough to have heard Washington or Lee. Scott had been almost a mile away. No one made such claims during Washington's lifetime, and even Lee never accused Washington of profanity. The transcript of Lee's subsequent court-martial reflected only a blunt battlefield exchange between the two senior commanders of the Continental Army, an occasion dramatic enough on its own, without after-the-fact embellishment.

As Washington confronted Lee, the British advance continued. Lee's troops still were struggling west, covered by Continental artillery that limbered up with the enemy only yards behind them. Washington quickly recognized the gravity of the British threat.

He ordered Wayne, with about 900 soldiers, to go into an area now known as the Point of Woods to the right of the British approach, and he tasked Lee with organizing a holding action west of Wayne's position. As Washington rode back to meet the main army, which was still coming up, Lee and Wayne feverishly prepared for the imminent British attack. Wayne's troops took cover behind any trees or terrain features they could find, as the thick woods did not permit a line. Lee formed behind a hedgerow directly in front of the British advance and about 850 yards west of Wayne's concealed soldiers. The hedgerow (the same one the militia had defended that morning against Simcoe) offered concealment but not much actual cover. Musket balls and bayonets could, and soon would, penetrate it easily. At least the Continentals could form a line. They also had artillery cover, as Henry Knox had come forward to join Lee and take charge of the guns that were retreating with Lee's infantry. Some of the most serious fighting of the war loomed.

As Wayne and Lee braced for battle, Washington made his way to Perrine Hill—the very place to which Lee had been headed. The commander in chief planned to make his stand on the heights, and he tasked Maj. Gen. William Alexander with arranging the arriving regiments and artillery. Alexander was a major New Jersey landowner who claimed he held a Scottish earldom and preferred to be called Lord Stirling, a title the Scots had accepted but which the House of Lords in London had rejected. This rejection had left Stirling with little love for Britain. Stirling placed some thirty guns along the crest of the hill, creating one of the largest concentrations of Continental artillery to date in the war, with all four of the army's artillery regiments represented. Most of the infantry was in position, just below the guns, along the military crest that gave maximum coverage of the battlefield. Washington rode up the hill, conspicuous as he encouraged his troops and no doubt hoping Wayne and Lee could hold long enough for him to establish a firm line, for he expected Clinton to come after him.

The rebels' main army was still taking its final position as the shooting started to the east. The advancing British had seen Lee forming at the hedgerow, but they had not seen Wayne scrambling into the woods. For that, the redcoats paid a stiff price. As the *1st Guards Battalion* marched by, heading for Lee, Wayne's Continentals blasted them at almost point-blank range. Staggered for an instant, the guards—the pride of the British army—accompanied by the *1st Grenadier Battalion* and the *16th Light Dragoons*, then stormed into the woods and into a ferocious hand-to-hand fight with Wayne's troops. The weight of British numbers and momentum quickly told on the rebels, and, under terrific pressure and suffering heavy casualties, Wayne's remnants pulled out. The staggered Continentals made for the bridge, passing to the left of Lee's position at the hedgerow, and headed for the safety of Perrine Hill.

The rest of the British, now breaking into a rush, made for Lee at the hedgerow. Clinton bravely but recklessly led from the front, swinging his sword and riding, as one of his junior officers recalled, "like a Newmarket jockey" and shouting for his soldiers to forget their formation and to charge flat-out for the rebels. They did, and the fighting at the hedgerow was brutal and short. Continentals and redcoats exchanged fire only feet from one another and thrust bayonets through the fence and foliage. At one point, a Continental officer leveled a pistol at Clinton, only to have one of the general's aides strike the assailant down at the last second. Among the patriots, Lt. Col. Alexander Hamilton and Lt. Col. John Laurens (son of Henry Laurens) were roughed up badly when their horses were shot out from under them. Lee watched the battle from a knoll directly behind the hedgerow in company with Knox, whose gun crews fired frantically in support of the infantry.

Intense and desperate as it was, the action at the hedgerow probably lasted only about ten minutes before Lee realized the British were gaining the upper hand. The redcoats who had forced Wayne from the Point of Woods now were working around Lee's left, and the *16th Light Dragoons*, having chased off the militia horse units, were closing on the rebel right. Flanked on both ends of his line, Lee ordered his soldiers to fall back over the bridge, which they did in good order. It had been a gallant defense against an equally gallant assault. Lee and Wayne had accomplished their mission: they had bought time for the commander in chief to bring up the main army and put it in a solid defensive posture.

The British made a final stab at the retreating patriots. As the last of Lee's troops escaped, Lt. Col. Henry Monckton led elements of the *2d Grenadier Battalion* on a charge across the bridge, while other grenadiers attempted to push across the bog and wade the stream. This may have been a spontaneous decision on Monckton's part, as there is no record of Clinton or Cornwallis ordering an attack across the west morass. In any case, it was a bad idea. The massed Continental guns on Perrine Hill scythed down the grenadiers with grape and canister. Brave though the grenadiers were, they did not stand a chance. Monckton fell, mortally wounded, the highest-ranking British casualty of the day. The rebels later found him and brought him to a field hospital on the grounds of the Tennent Meetinghouse, where his grave is today. The charge was over in a horrible minute. Of all the British troops, the grenadiers had come the closest to what had become the center of Washington's main line, but they now lay in heaps, both dead and wounded (*Map 6*).

Other royal troops had tried and failed on the Continental left. Grey's brigade had moved quickly, and the *42d Foot* had caught up with some of Scott's retreating Continentals. There was scattered firing, but Scott made it to the patriot left on Perrine Hill. Facing rebel artillery, Grey's assault stalled, and the brigade took cover in an orchard. They kept their heads down as Stirling's guns peppered them with grapeshot. Erskine's light infantry and rangers fared no better. Confronted with artillery and a patriot infantry reserve forming behind Stirling, Erskine's soldiers pulled back to the Sutfin and Craig farms on the right of Grey. Like Grey's men, they suffered in the scorching heat, further plagued by a rebel 4-pounder firing grape. Thus, for the time being, there was little action on the rebel left.

The defeat of Monckton's grenadiers and the stalled British attacks of Grey and Erskine marked a lull in the action. The rebels had consolidated their position on Perrine Hill, while Clinton pulled back to the hedgerow Lee recently had defended. Unknown

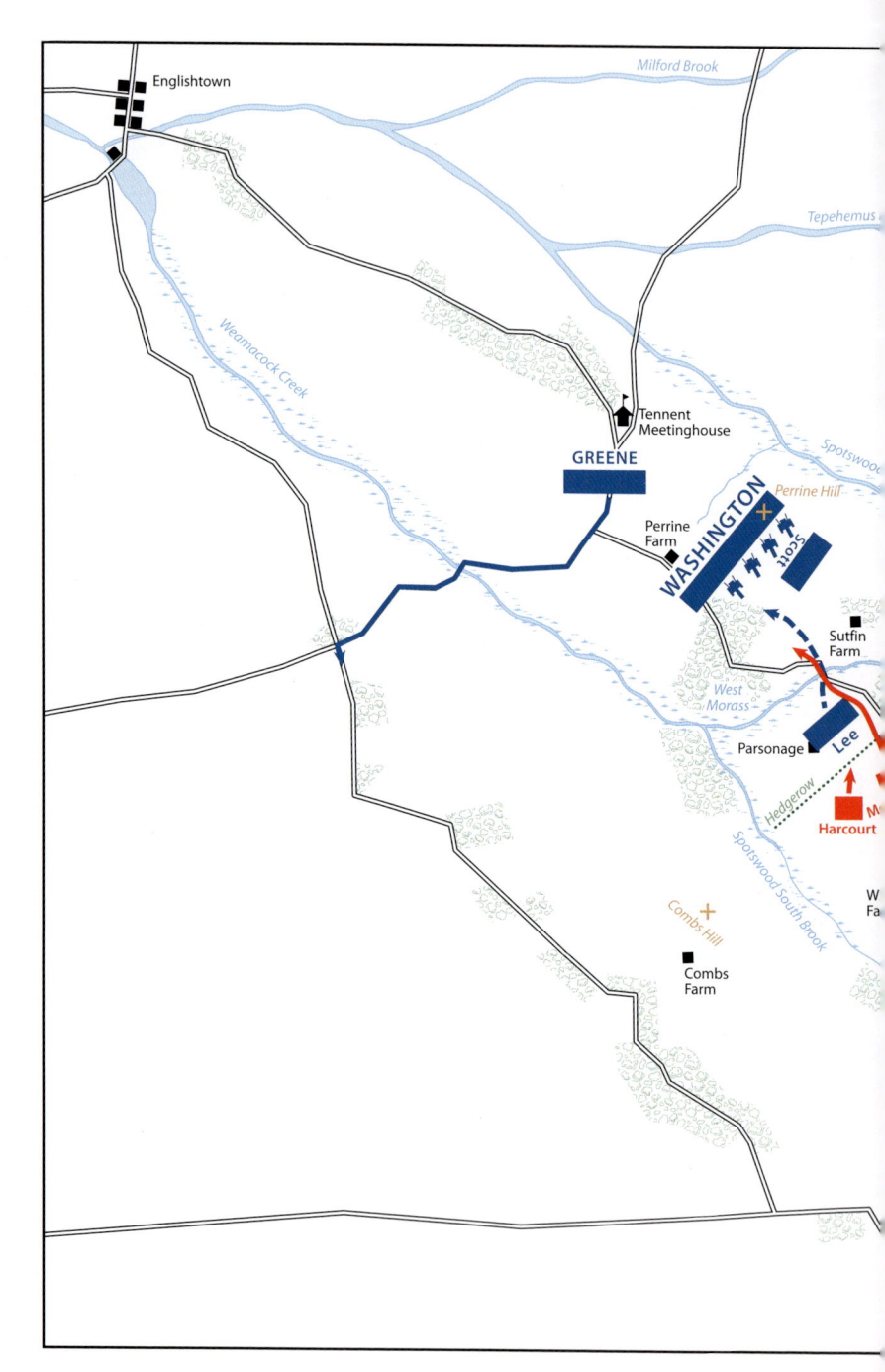

Map 6

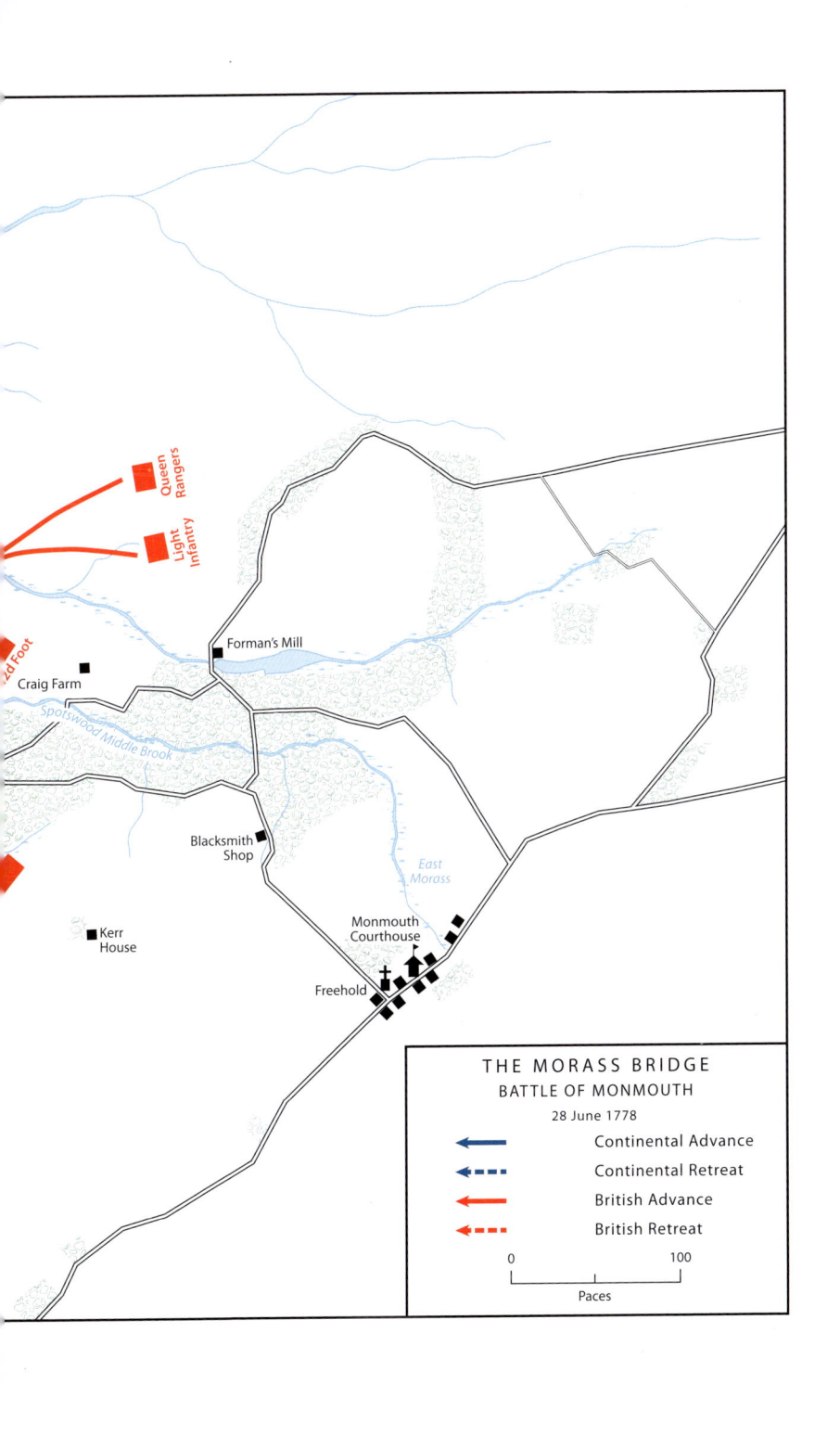

THE MORASS BRIDGE
BATTLE OF MONMOUTH
28 June 1778

← Continental Advance
←-- Continental Retreat
← British Advance
←-- British Retreat

0 — 100
Paces

to Clinton, the Continental detachment with four guns under Nathanael Greene was slowly working its way from Washington's right, aiming to get in position on Clinton's left, though it would be some time before Greene could engage. Meanwhile, both main armies got what rest they could. Troops on both sides had endured a brutally hot morning and early afternoon. Combat had raged in temperatures well above 90 degrees, and the humidity held clouds of smoke in the air. Heat exhaustion proved as dangerous as enemy fire and likely accounted for additional casualties.

It was now about 1345, and for the moment, the infantry battle was over—but not the artillery fight. Rival Continental and *Royal Artillery* batteries slugged it out in one of the longest continuous cannonades of the war. Rebel gun crews, reequipped and reorganized at Valley Forge under Knox, proved as good as their veteran British opponents. The opposing gunners actually fought in line of sight. For all of the sound and fury, however, and for all of the hot metal flung through the torrid air, neither side inflicted much damage compared with the pitched infantry battle. Awed rebel infantry, in positions below Knox's artillery line, looked on as the gun crews fired over their heads. It was a spectacular show.

During the cannonade, a camp follower stepped out of obscurity and into American folklore. The camp follower was almost certainly Mary Ludwig Hays, the wife of artillerist William Hays, who was serving in Colonel Procter's regiment (designated the 4th Continental Artillery Regiment in 1779). Mary had followed William into the army during the Philadelphia Campaign, and she followed him again from Valley Forge to the Monmouth battlefield. As her moniker "Molly Pitcher" (bestowed upon her in the nineteenth century) suggests, Hays was bringing water from a nearby spring either to relieve the thirsty gun crews or, perhaps more likely, to swab the guns between rounds. Legend has it that, when William collapsed in the brutal heat, Mary took his place with the crew at the cannon.

Although historians can verify neither this legend nor a soldier's supposedly eyewitness account, recorded decades after the battle, of a British cannonball blowing off her petticoat as it passed harmlessly between her legs, Mary would have been one of at least several women

Molly Pitcher, engraving by J. C. Armytage after Alonzo Chappel, ca. 1859 (*Library of Congress*)

on the field who served in similar supporting roles during combat. Their presence was further, and ample, testimony to the integral place of women with the Continental army.

Almost by some unstated mutual consent, the fire lifted about 1545. With the afternoon lengthening, and the heat not letting up, Clinton decided to call it a day. Convinced Washington would not offer a general action, and with his baggage train safely away, he concluded it was time to pull out and head to Sandy Hook.

Washington, however, had other plans. Feeling secure from attack, he decided to risk some limited offensives. He sent two battalions of picked men to clear the redcoats from the orchard on the patriot left. Only the battalion of about 275 soldiers under Col. Joseph Cilley of New Hampshire engaged. Taking advantage of covering terrain, Cilley approached the *42d Foot* unobserved, then swung his platoons into line and advanced. It was a deftly executed surprise that illustrated the Continentals' maturing tactical capabilities. The startled highlanders responded like professionals and formed to confront Cilley. The numbers were about equal, but the *42d Foot* was on poor ground and withdrew as the rebels closed. Cilley sent a platoon or two to skirmish with the withdrawing *Black Watch* while the rest of the battalion advanced in formation. The skirmishers pursued "in no order," harassing the British with musketry, but the veteran highlanders were not flustered. When they reached higher ground, they fired a long-range volley and then continued their retrograde.

Cilley's soldiers, knocking down a fence, advanced with shouldered arms. The fighting then intensified as the *42d* reformed along the edge of a swamp, and some British light infantry arrived to cover the highlanders with two 3-pounders. Cilley's unit came on as the 3-pounders opened on them, and the *42d* fired volleys of musketry. Unwilling to slow down while under artillery fire, the rebel battalion "got within 4 rods of them [the British]," recalled Lt. Col. Henry Dearborn. Then, he continued, "our men dressed very coolly and we gave them a very heavy fire from the whole battalion." The Continentals advanced between volleys with "charged bayonet" and took losses. Pvt. Joseph Plumb Martin graphically described the deadly results of a ball from one of the British 3-pounders, recollecting, "The first shot they gave us . . . cut off the thigh bone of a captain, just above the knee [a mortal wound], and the whole heel of a private in the rear of him."

At this point, the commander of the *42d* saw no point in continuing the contest. The highlanders had bought time for the light infantry, the *Queen's American Rangers*, and the rest of Grey's brigade to pull back toward Clinton's position near the hedgerow. Thus, about 1700, the Scots withdrew in a fighting retrograde, with the Continentals following. Private Martin remembered Cilley shouting for his troops to reload and fire a final volley. "We did so," Martin recalled, "and gave them the parting salute." Cilley later regretted not pursuing the British further, but he explained that "the extreme heat" was so bad that it had killed several of his soldiers. The brief action was over. The British dismissed the fighting as inconsequential, but rebel morale soared, and Washington was delighted.

Cilley's engagement was noteworthy. The colonel's battalion was a temporary formation of picked men. Most did not know one another or their officers, much less Cilley, who initially had trouble even identifying some of the troops ordered to join him. Nevertheless, this group of soldiers from many different regiments had executed a flawless movement to contact, had formed, and had fired in volley like the uniformly trained troops they now were. Without Steuben's common regimen, would such an amalgam of soldiery have functioned as a coherent unit? Success depended on officers and their troops knowing what to do in unison, and that meant following a shared and practiced drill. Cilley's action with the *42d Foot* may have been a small battle, but it was a telling demonstration of the effectiveness of Steuben's tutelage (*Map 7*).

As his light infantry and Grey's brigade were disengaging, Clinton felt he could pull back, mission accomplished. He ordered a phased withdrawal toward the village. The grenadier battalions were to stay in position near the hedgerow until Grey and the light troops were out of danger. The maneuver, however, misfired. "From my instructions not being properly understood," Clinton explained, all units but the *1st Grenadier Battalion* pulled out right away. This premature withdrawal left Grey's still retreating brigade lagging behind on the British right and left the *1st Grenadier Battalion* isolated at the hedgerow.

Here, Washington may have seen an opportunity. The view from Perrine Hill allowed only glimpses of British movements, but it was clear the redcoats had retreated on the rebel left, and the patriots knew that the enemy artillery had pulled out. Were the British vulnerable near the hedgerow? Lacking any solid intelligence, Washington risked another limited advance. He sent Wayne with the 3d Pennsylvania Brigade (some 500 soldiers) back over the west morass bridge. The commander in chief had no specific target in mind; Wayne was to advance from the Continental center and pursue any advantage.

Wayne was aggressive, even with only a brigade. He marched about 1645, while Cilley was still pursuing the highlanders. Wayne's forces were fresh, and they advanced swiftly, although their exact

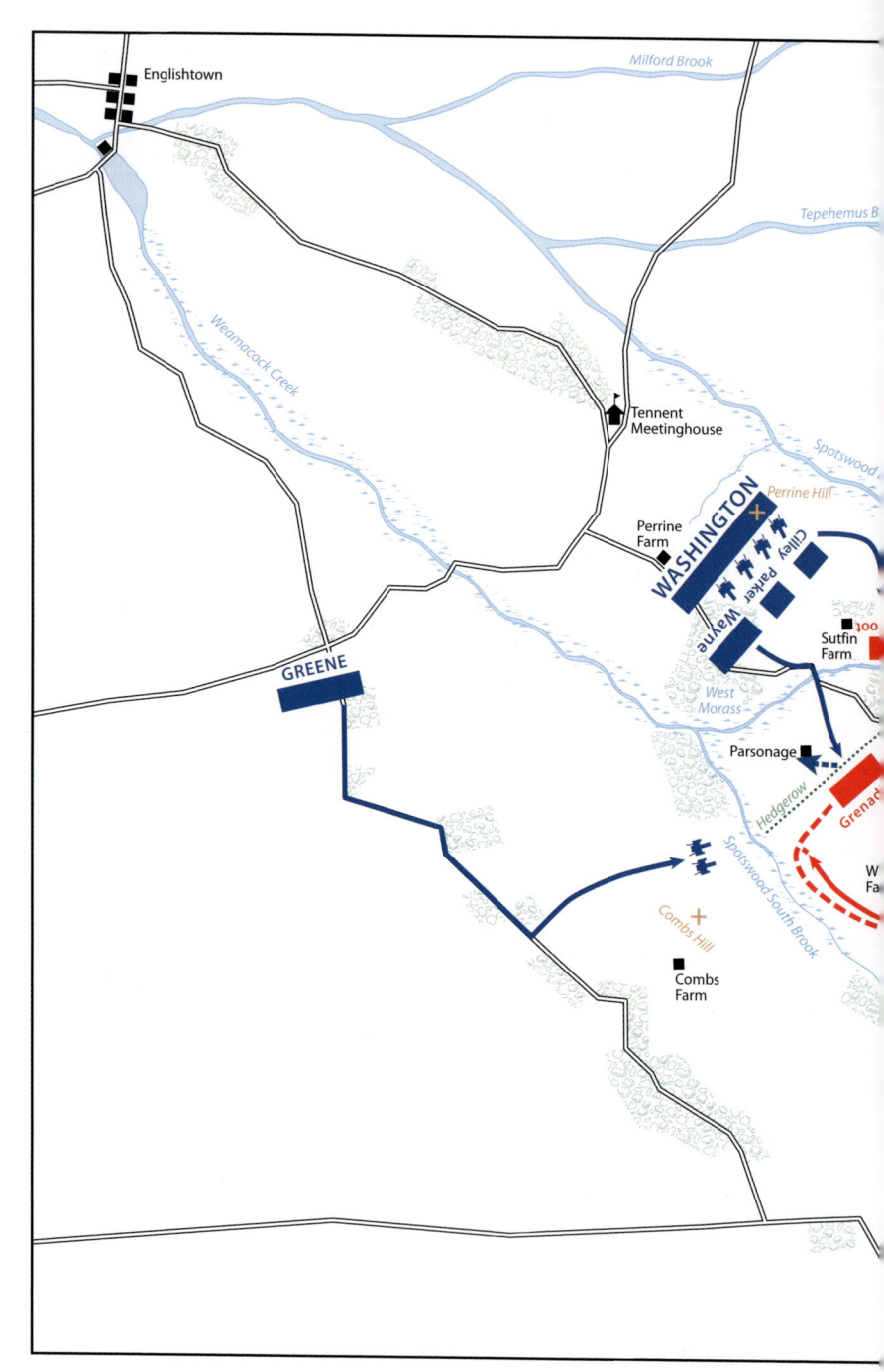

Map 7

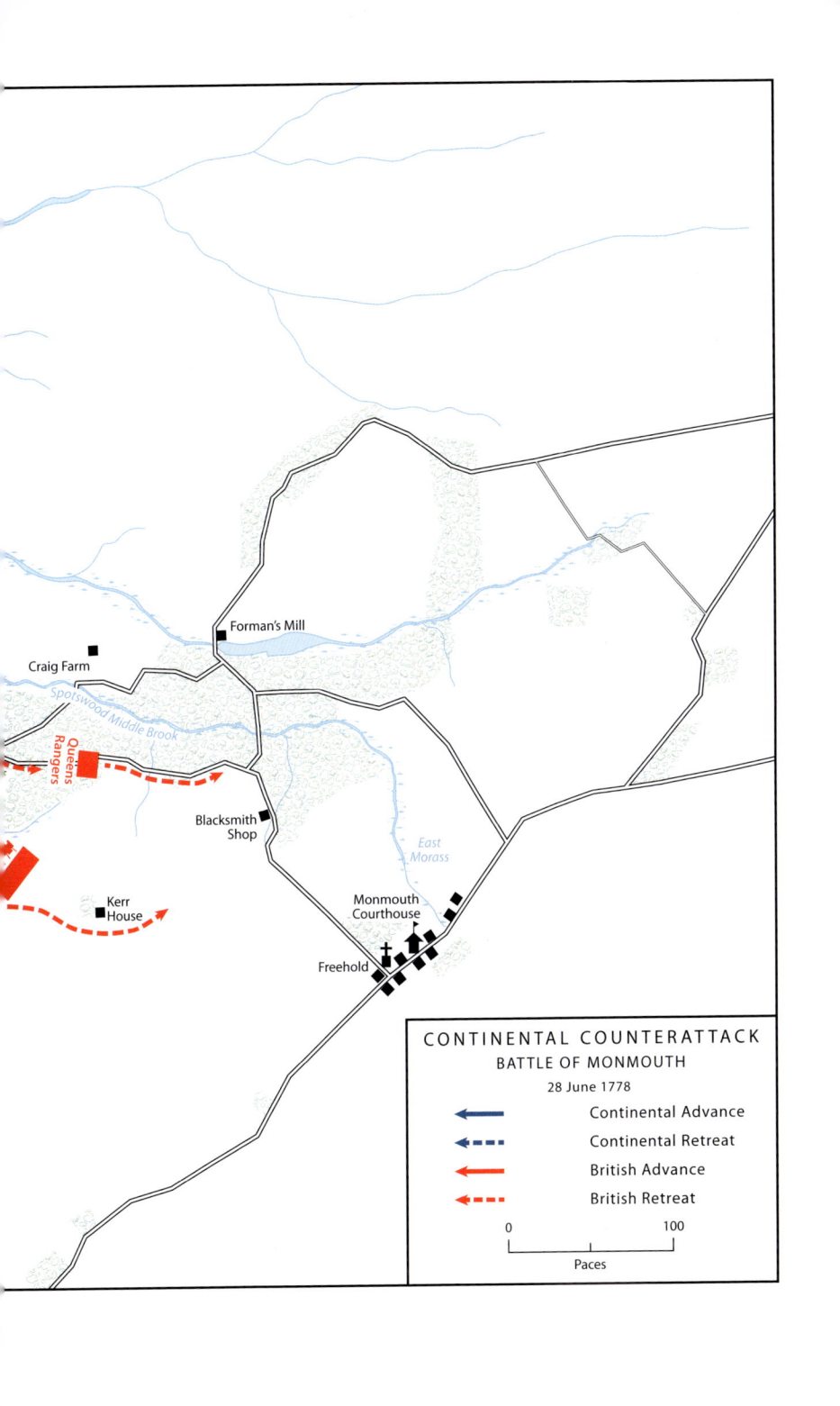

Craig Farm
Forman's Mill
Spotswood Middle Brook
Queens Rangers
Blacksmith Shop
Kerr House
East Morass
Monmouth Courthouse
Freehold

CONTINENTAL COUNTERATTACK
BATTLE OF MONMOUTH
28 June 1778

← Continental Advance
←-- Continental Retreat
← British Advance
←-- British Retreat

0   100
Paces

movements are conjectural. They certainly crossed the west morass bridge unopposed and likely made it to the hedgerow area without incident. Then, as they moved past the hedgerow, they spotted the *1st Grenadier Battalion*, who had just withdrawn. Wayne hit them hard with three volleys, probably before the grenadiers could form fully. The grenadiers, who earlier had been shot up badly in the Point of Woods, were now unsupported, but they rallied and fought back gamely. "This brave corps," Clinton wrote of the *1st Grenadier Battalion*, began "losing men very fast." Wayne was in his glory.

Clinton had not anticipated the Continental movement, but he quickly sized up the threat. The Continentals had come over the bridge "in great force," he noted, and riding close to the scene, he saw no alternative but to stand and fight. In some anxiety, the general searched the field for additional reinforcements. Fortuitously, Sir Henry spotted the *33d Foot* moving up. The regimental commander, Lt. Col. James Webster, apparently was heading for the sound of the guns on his own initiative, and Clinton sent Webster's troops immediately into the fray.

The subsequent action may have been the bitterest of the day. Numbers were now against the Continentals. Wayne was facing roughly 1,000 redcoats, who had the advantage of both strength and spirit. Formed in semiopen order, the British line threatened to flank the patriots. According to traditional accounts, Wayne remained cool as the British gathered momentum. He told his troops to hold their fire; he wanted the grenadiers and the *33d* to get within range of a sure kill and then have the Continentals go for the enemy officers. "Steady, steady," the general supposedly called down his line, "wait for the word, then pick out the King birds."

The patriot volley slowed but did not stop the redcoat advance, and Wayne began a withdrawal. Pushed back through the hedgerow, Wayne's formation began to disintegrate as Continentals hurried to take cover in the buildings and enclosures of a nearby parsonage and farm. Terrain sheltered the pursuing grenadiers from the Continental artillery on Perrine Hill, but they had no protection from the Continentals at the parsonage. Behind fences and walls, the rebels were safe from a bayonet charge. A grenadier officer reported that his soldiers had "lost Considerable [killed and wounded] from a Firing from a Barn & a House." The redcoats came on, loading and firing, but their advance was short-lived.

Enter Nathanael Greene, who had been following roads from Washington's right for more than three hours. With him was French artillerist Thomas-Antoine de Mauduit du Plessis and four cannons. Around 1600, Greene reached Combs Hill, a striking terrain feature that that overlooked the battlefield and was eminently defensible. In fact, before heading for Perrine Hill in the morning, Lee had considered occupying Combs Hill, but swampy ground at the hill's base had discouraged the idea. As an artillery position, the high ground was perfect. Until the battle with Wayne brought them into the open, terrain largely had protected the *1st Grenadier Battalion* from the hill. Now, however, du Plessis had a clear target, and the redcoats were sitting ducks.

Du Plessis sent a withering rain of shot ripping through Clinton's left flank, replaying Monckton's tragic fate at the west morass bridge. Trained gun crews could fire two or three aimed rounds per minute. A 4-pounder grapeshot round contained about forty-four 1.5-ounce iron spheres, while a canister round held a larger number of lead musket balls. With all four guns firing at a rate of three rounds per minute, more than 500 pieces of hot metal were hurtling downrange at any given minute, aimed at infantry in enfilade. Multiple hits were as likely as not. The artillery storm staggered the redcoats, who were powerless to reply. Virtually every account of this action, whether patriot or British, bore testimony to the terrible effectiveness of the fire from Combs Hill. The British attack ended almost immediately. The grenadiers and the *33d* quickly retreated, and once they were east of the hedgerow, the topography hid them from du Plessis.

In a technical sense, Clinton had won the fight with Wayne—the Continentals had retreated—but his grenadiers and the *33d* were licking their wounds as they moved out. The weary troops withdrew about a half mile to high ground near the Kerr house, arriving shortly after 1800 for some much needed rest. The British withdrawal from the parsonage area marked the end of the day's longest period of sustained infantry action. Clinton rightly suspected that Washington would be willing to venture only relatively small forays, so he saw no reason to further delay his march to Sandy Hook. He planned to leave after the division was rested and to catch up with Knyphausen.

For Washington, however, the day was not over. Clinton's retrograde invited a response, and he planned a final blow. Around 1800, the commander in chief ordered Steuben to bring what troops he could from Englishtown. Lee's soldiers were there, but they were in terrible condition after their long day in the sun; Lee himself was too exhausted for further duty. Nevertheless, Steuben had three fresh brigades—more than 1,800 troops. They arrived at Perrine Hill too late for combat on Sunday, but they would be at hand if fighting resumed on Monday. Shortly after 1800 on Sunday the twenty-eighth, Washington ordered two columns to go after Clinton's flanks. The first was under General Poor of New Hampshire, who took his own brigade, a detachment of North Carolinians, and a picked body of light infantry. Poor had a reputation as a steady officer, and he had been with Stirling during the earlier fighting. He was to cross the west morass bridge to go after Clinton's right. Moving in concert with Poor would be the small Virginia Brigade of Brig. Gen. William Woodford. Woodford had been with Greene on Combs Hill, and his unit had covered du Plessis's guns. He would advance from the hill and try for the British left. Knox limbered up guns to accompany Poor.

Poor crossed the bridge and moved carefully through fields and patches of woods, seeking to conceal his advance. Woodford picked his way through the boggy terrain at the base of Combs Hill. Unsure of how far they could go before the British saw them or of how the redcoats would react, caution ruled their approaches. The pace was too slow, and sunset halted the advance. Washington had these troops lie on their arms close enough to the Kerr house to keep an eye on the enemy. Behind Poor and Woodford, some troops from Stirling's brigades moved to positions near the hedgerow, "lying down on the field amongst the dead." On Perrine Hill, Steuben's fresh troops replaced Stirling's soldiers. Washington, who fully intended to renew the fighting on Monday morning, slept under an oak, sharing a cloak with Lafayette.

The infantry of the two armies rested within a mile of each other, but their only contact during the evening was when a company of picked men attempted to disturb the redcoats' sleep. They probed forward until they found an enemy picket, fired three volleys, and returned unscathed. Other than return fire from the picket, the only opposition Washington's troops encountered were a few bursting shells from British 5½-inch howitzers. In an effort to keep the Continentals at a distance, Clinton had his artillerists randomly fire at the ground he had abandoned.

Clinton let his exhausted units rest, secure in their temporary camp. His intention was to join Knyphausen, who by 1800, had marched the baggage train and its escorts to a defensible encampment at Nut Swamp, which was well beyond Monmouth Courthouse and some 3 miles from the village of Middletown, New Jersey, which itself was about 11 miles from Sandy Hook. Around midnight, Clinton quietly broke camp, slipped into the night, and left the battlefield to Washington. Poor's men never heard him go. The withdrawal was skillful and efficient (every bit as good as Washington's escape from Cornwallis after the Second Battle of Trenton), but the exhausted and sleeping rebels would have been unprepared to stop Clinton even if they had noticed his departure.

Not all the redcoats left. The British left four officers and forty soldiers, all wounded too badly to be moved, in the village. They remained under the care of medical personnel who volunteered to stay behind. To Maj. John André, it was "mortifying" to leave their wounded to the rebels, but there was nothing else to be done. Even if the wounded troops were in good enough condition to travel, there were not enough wagons to carry them, most of the wagons having departed with Knyphausen. Clinton trusted that Washington would treat the wounded humanely, and in this he was not disappointed; patriot medical personnel did all they could to assist the redcoats.

At Nut Swamp, Knyphausen awaited his chief, having arrived without the loss of a single wagon. The German general had avoided the direct road to Middletown; instead, he had marched farther

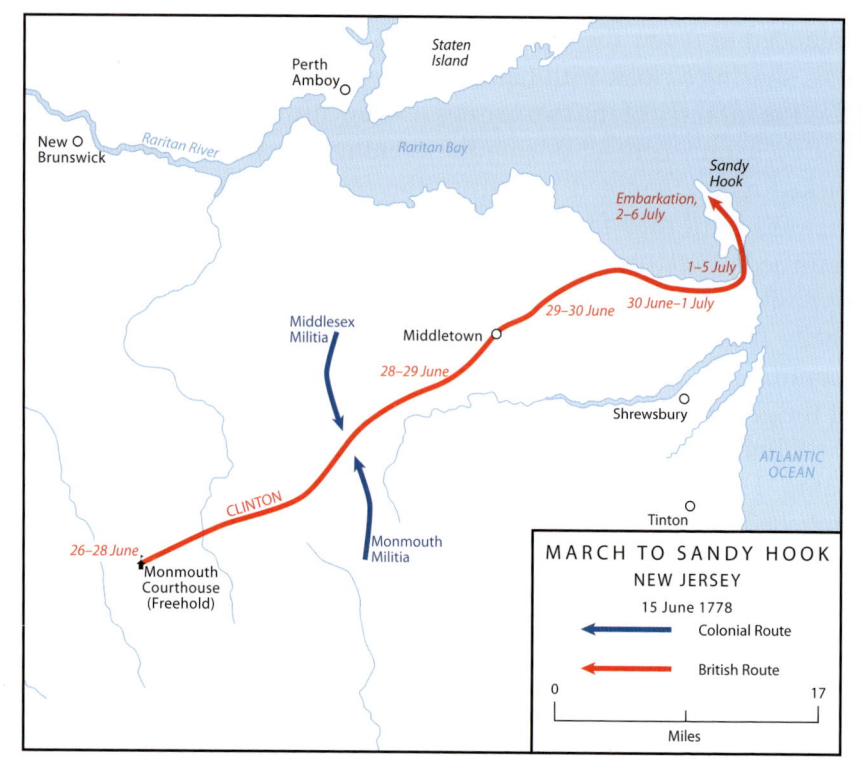

Map 8

east, largely throwing the militia off his track. Had he traveled the routes the rebels expected, a frustrated militia colonel lamented, a "great part of their Baggage must have fallen into our hands." The Hessian avoided major fighting, but John Hills, the British engineer who had risked his life to provide route intelligence for Clinton, noted three militia attacks. Two were brushes with the dragoon escort. However, a third was more serious. Capt. Joshua Huddy of the Monmouth County militia found a gap in Knyphausen's flank guards and launched a wild bayonet attack on the baggage, stabbing horses, beating drivers with musket butts, and even overturning a few wagons. In the confused firing, two women who had been marching with the baggage were killed, one with a baby in her arms. The baggage guards quickly routed the militia, killing two and chasing the others into a swamp. Another militia company hurried to the sound of the guns and ran straight into the sabers of the *17th Light Dragoons*. The horsemen killed three and wounded another in a vicious encounter. These were pinprick attacks, but they were harrowing for those involved.

Clinton, after marching all night, joined Knyphausen by 0900 on 29 June. The following day, the British marched to the Navesink Highlands overlooking Sandy Hook. The hook was a loyalist stronghold and hosted a considerable refugee population, including active raiders who struck at patriot targets mostly in Monmouth County. For the moment, Clinton allowed his exhausted soldiers to get some badly needed rest on the highlands. He used the time to prepare the complicated logistics of moving thousands of troops, camp followers, wagons, and tons of equipment to the hook and embarking for the New York area. (Most horses simply would be turned loose.) He sent patrols back toward Middletown to discourage patriot harassment. On 5 July, Clinton moved the bulk of his command to Sandy Hook while a security force remained on the highlands (*Map 8*). By the sixth, the *Royal Navy* had ferried the army to safety in positions on Staten Island, Long Island, and Manhattan Island, New York. For the British, the campaign was over.

As Clinton pulled away, Washington chose not to give chase. His army was also tired and needed to regroup after the fighting. He did send Morgan—who finally was back in touch—to shadow Clinton's march, but nothing of consequence came out of it. In the meantime, most of the 1,500–2,000 militia members in the field went home, and Washington consolidated at Englishtown. By 2 July, the Continentals had reached New Brunswick after a scorching march; by the sixth, most of the army occupied positions in the Hudson Highlands across from New York. The New Jersey Brigade remained in New Jersey in posts opposite New York City and British-occupied Staten Island. After more than two years of war, the rival armies essentially were back where they had been in late 1776.

This stasis was not lost on the rebel commander in chief. Just more than a month after Monmouth, Washington wrote to an old friend. Thomas Nelson, another member of Virginia's planter elite, was a militia brigadier general and, in the future, would become governor. Washington, confiding to his social equal, provided his concluding thoughts on the campaign, expressing what he probably would not have said publicly:

> It is not a little pleasing nor less wonderful to contemplate, that after two long years Manoeuvring and undergoing the strangest vicissitudes that perhaps ever attended any one contest since the creation both Armies are brought back to the very point they set out from and, that that, which was the offending party in the beginning is now reduced to the use of the spade and pick axe for the defence. The hand of Providence has been so conspicuous in all this, that he must be worse than an infidel that lacks faith, and more than wicked, that has not gratitude enough to acknowledge his obligations, but, it will be time enough for me to turn preacher, when my present appointment ceases.

ANALYSIS

The morning of 29 June found the rebels jubilant. "It is Glorious for America," Col. Israel Shreve exclaimed to his wife, for the "Enemy was Drove off the Ground." In "all the actions hitherto," crowed Col. William Irvine, a tough Pennsylvanian, patriots had never held the field, but this time they had humbled "the pride of the British Tyrant." In near disbelief, another officer informed his wife that "Our little boys" had bested "their Gigantic Grenadiers." Political reactions were similar. John Hancock, the former congressional president, proclaimed that the battle had "Ruin'd" the British, while Connecticut delegate Titus Hosmer rejoiced at the supposedly disastrous state of the enemy. Henry Laurens, who privately viewed the battle as a "partial Victory gained over our Enemies," publicly was delighted at Washington's performance. Much of Congress believed Clinton narrowly had avoided Burgoyne's fate, and on 7 July, the delegates thanked Washington and his army for "gaining the important victory at Monmouth [Courthouse] over the British grand army." Few rebels doubted that Monmouth had left the British reeling.

Patriot euphoria, of course, was an overreaction; at best, the claims of victory had been overstated. After all, as his orders demanded, Clinton had led his army safely back to New York, and he had done so without the loss of a single wagon. Nevertheless, after the setbacks of 1777, Washington wanted—and politically *needed*—credit for more than a tactical draw. Thus, Washington began crafting a victory narrative for public consumption. On 29 June, he briefly informed Congress he had forced "the Enemy from the Field." Further specifics followed on 1 July in the general's first detailed after action report since the calamities of 1777. Carefully understated, Washington's letter limned the course of the campaign, the ferocity of the fighting, the punishing heat, the gallantry of the troops, and Clinton's departure from the field. The conclusion was unambiguous: Monmouth had been a triumph, and the revived Continental Army—and Washington as its commander—had passed the test of combat. The general had redeemed the disappointments of 1777.

Washington's friends saw Monmouth as a final blow to the commander in chief's erstwhile critics. Elias Boudinot, the army's commissary general of prisoners, wrote to Hamilton, "the General I always revered & loved . . . has rose superior to himself. Every Lip dwells on his Praise for even his pretended friends (for none dare to acknowledge themselves his Enemies) are obliged to croak it forth." So much for the Conway Cabal. Hamilton agreed. "You know my way of thinking about our army," he told Boudinot, "and I am not about to flatter it. I assure you I never was pleased with them before this day." In fact, Hamilton and fellow Washington aide John Laurens had worked hard to spin the Monmouth story favorably. Laurens had written to his influential father, complimenting Washington and casting aspersions on Lee's conduct. Hamilton had done the same with anyone who would listen. The story was consistent: Washington had won the day; only Lee's retreat had prevented Clinton's destruction. The public got the message.

Dealing with Charles Lee was central to the Monmouth victory narrative. A known critic of the commander in chief, Lee was already unpopular with much of the officer corps, and his retreat on the twenty-eighth gave rise to sniping from Washington's partisans. Frankly, these verbal attacks amounted to character assassination. Lee had fought well at Monmouth Courthouse, but it seemed his fate would have more to do with politics than the battlefield. The commander in chief disliked his chief subordinate, but despite his battlefield exchange with Lee, there is little indication that Washington envisioned any postbattle action against him. Still, the circulating gossip offended Lee, and he wrote two snarky letters to Washington insisting on a court-martial to clear himself of rumored misconduct. Washington complied, and Lee stood accused on three counts: failing to attack on 28 June "agreeable to repeated instructions"; leading "an *unnecessary, disorderly,* and *shameful retreat*"; and disrespecting the commander in chief in his letters after the battle. The first two charges were preposterous, but the third held water. Lee indeed had been disrespectful to Washington, and that finished him. It would not be possible for the court to find Lee guilty only of the third count, because, as historian John Shy notes, "under the circumstances, an acquittal on the first two charges would have been a vote of no-confidence in Washington." Thus, the guilty verdicts were no surprise, although the court did delete the word "shameful" from the second count. The court suspended Lee from the service for a year, and Washington forwarded the verdict to Congress. The delegates, however, were in no hurry to deal with the hot-button matter.

The delay gave partisans of Washington and Lee plenty of time to lobby for their favorites, and Lee did garner a measure of public sympathy. However, on 5 December, after months of waiting and suspense, Congress resolved to sustain the verdict. It had no choice. Congress could not risk the army's welfare to offer justice to one man. Either Lee or Washington would have to goand it was *not* going to be Washington. Even so, the vote was not unanimous. Of the twenty-three delegates, seven believed Lee had been wronged. Rather than accept his suspension, Lee left the army in disgust. His disgrace virtually silenced further public criticisms of the commander in chief.

Sir Henry Clinton gave no indication that he cared about the politics of the rebel army, but he scoffed at the rebels' proclamations of a Monmouth victory and their claims that he barely had avoided being "Burgoyned." He correctly noted that he had done what he had set out to do: he had successfully returned his troops to New York. From there, the British proceeded with their army's redeployment. The events at Monmouth Courthouse had had no impact on the implementation of the empire's strategy.

As for the battle itself, Washington's Continentals never defeated Sir Henry's army. Once Clinton determined he could not bring on a general engagement, he had no interest in prolonging the contest. Exactly when Clinton realized there was no value in continuing that battle remains hazy. Was it when Grey and Erskine failed to turn the patriot left? When Monckton came to grief across the west morass? Or when the *Royal Artillery* failed to silence the Continental guns? Cilley's clash with the highlanders, no matter how satisfying to the rebels, was a push against troops who already were retiring. The *1st Grenadier Battalion* and the *33d Foot* suffered cruelly at the hands of Wayne's infantry and the guns of du Plessis, but the Continentals failed to disrupt Clinton's withdrawal. Britain's superiority in cavalry and its excellent light infantry, including the Hessian jaeger, provided outstanding protection for the major troop formations and the baggage train. The high order of British professionalism was evident throughout the campaign.

Still, as professionals, the British were cognizant of their opponent's gritty performance. The Continentals had done well, and British officers admitted as much. They recognized not just rebel tenacity—they had seen plenty of that in the past—but also the improved tactical proficiency of Washington's army. "The Enemy were very troublesom" at Monmouth Courthouse, a junior officer conceded. The rebels had left his regiment "a good dale cut up." William Erskine, one of Clinton's ablest brigadiers, reported the battle as "a handsome flogging. We had not receiv'd such an one in America." Andrew Bell, Clinton's secretary, candidly admitted "the Rebels stood much better than ever they did." Despite its flaws, the Continental Army had earned the grudging respect of some of Europe's best soldiers.

Whatever their perspective on the battle's outcome, everyone involved recognized that the entire campaign had been punishing. Washington officially tallied 69 patriot dead, 161 wounded, and 141 missing after Monmouth. Postbattle losses from wounds, heat, and disease likely increased patriot casualties to 450–500 killed, wounded, and missing. Clinton's losses totaled well more than 300 killed (including those who died from the heat) and considerably more wounded. In addition, a fair number of British soldiers were captured, and as many as 1,000 deserted during the march from Philadelphia. Altogether, the cost was substantial.

Even though the campaign, including Monmouth, was not a decisive encounter in a strategic sense, it was nevertheless revealing. The army that fought Sir Henry at Monmouth Courthouse was much better than the army that had fought William Howe the year before. Indeed, a number of historians have seen the Battle of Monmouth as the "coming of age" of the Continental Line, although the point deserves scrutiny.

After Monmouth, few contemporaries believed that the Continental infantry could match the tactical finesse of the British, but many generally agreed that the Continentals had performed admirably. There is less accord, however, regarding the reasons behind this improvement. Some historians have questioned the extent to which Steuben's reforms were responsible. Was Steuben's training the key, or did Monmouth simply reflect the accumulated experience of two years of war? In fact, it is not an either-or question. The Prussian certainly had improved morale at Valley Forge, where he successfully introduced uniform drill and enhanced tactical performance. The Battle of Monmouth, however, presented few opportunities for the linear deployments integral to Steuben's instruction. Attacks by Lee, Cilley, and Wayne involved relatively small units, and, except for Cilley's, even these actions ended with the Continentals parrying enemy attacks. Indeed, the only general who mounted a major offensive operation on 28 June was Clinton. Washington let the British come to him, and rebel artillery accounted for most redcoat casualties. The patriot general never fought a major engagement in the open field.

Yet the impact of Valley Forge training *was* visible. True, no general action demonstrated improved Continental prowess, but the proficiency of the regulars was evident. The Continental infantry under Lee and Cilley consisted of picked men, drawn from any number of regiments and organized in temporary battalions. Many—probably *most*—of these soldiers had not served together previously, but their common bond was the training experience under Steuben. Officers needed to know the proper commands at the proper times, and they needed to know that their troops, whom they never had met, could react promptly to those commands. The alternative to this common understanding was chaos, which never occurred. During Lee's advance on Monmouth Courthouse, units shifted routinely from column to line and back again—a key element of Steuben's drill—and made proper use of the flanking skirmishers. Even criticisms of Lee's retreat were backhanded compliments; the complaints dealt less with confusion in the ranks than with columns marching too closely to swing easily on line. It was a given that the units knew what the proper maneuvers were. The same can be said of Cilley's ability to mount his afternoon attack. It was an advance in battalion strength, again with picked men, and again the rebels displayed considerable competence. At the very least, Steuben's training can be credited with enabling officers to maintain control under quite trying circumstances, which is no mean feat.

The Continental artillery was the province of Henry Knox, and certainly it was a force to reckon with at Monmouth Courthouse. Rebel cannoneers demonstrated a proficiency for quick deployment, company-level and massed-battery operations against infantry and the *Royal Artillery*, and courage and discipline in conducting maneuvers in the open. It was quite a performance. "My brave Lads behav'd with their usual intrepidity," Knox wrote to his wife, "& the Army give the Corps of Artillery their full proportion of the Glory of the day." The commander in chief was unstinting in his praise, specifically mentioning the artillery's valor and effectiveness in general orders. "No Artillery," he told the army, "could be better served than ours." He was right, for at Monmouth Courthouse, and for the rest of the war, the patriot gunners were as good as their counterparts in the *Royal Artillery*.

Less visible, but hardly less important, was a sterling rebel logistics effort. The work of Greene and Wadsworth paid major dividends; they both spared no efforts in supplying Washington. It was not easy. "I had the whole machinary of the Army to put in motion," Greene recalled, "Supplies of all kinds to attend to; Camps to look out; Routes to f[ind;] orders of march to furnish the General officers." Yet, from the time the army left Valley Forge, the troops seldom lacked food, forage, munitions, or other necessities. The only real exception occurred during Lafayette's ill-fated advance on 26 June, when provisions failed to reach advance units. Greene and Wadsworth spent lavishly to keep their departments running, but they got what they paid for. Rarely, if ever, had the supply services worked so smoothly in support of the combat arms during active operations.

Senior Continental leadership earned mixed marks. The army was fortunate in its commander in chief, for, on balance, Washington did well. Although he brought up the main body too slowly on the morning of 28 June, Washington took firm control when he arrived at the front. He issued orders decisively and used his subordinates effectively. For example, he used Lee and Wayne to fight the delaying action east of the west morass, Stirling to build the main line on the Perrine Hill, and Greene to occupy Combs Hill. His decision to send

Cilley and Wayne forward displayed aggressiveness while risking little. Ordering Woodford and Poor to advance at the end of the day allowed him to claim the battlefield and a morale-building boast of victory. He managed all this without theatrics. His defensive battle required steadiness, not daring. He never assumed a dual role as both commander in chief and tactical commander, that is, he presided over the battle and had no need to lead men, personally, into the fray. The general had sought a limited engagement that would enhance his stature and pay political dividends, and he had gotten it.

Washington was conspicuous during the fighting. His coolness as he rode the lines during the artillery barrage was inspirational. According to Lafayette, the general's "nobility, grace, and presence of mind were never displayed to better advantage." Washington's military secretary, James McHenry, remembered that he did "not think, for [his] part" that "the general in one day displayed more military powers, or acquired more real reputation. He gave a new turn to the action . . . examining the enemies manoeuvers—exhorting the troops—and directing the operation of his plans, He unfolded surprising abilities, which produced uncommon effects." McHenry and Lafayette spoke for many others who saw Monmouth as one of Washington's finest hours.

Washington's conduct was in stark contrast to that of his opponent. Clinton led from the front, exhorting his troops and exposed to enemy fire. If any rank and file heard him, perhaps they admired him for asking no more of them than he risked himself. Grey thought Clinton's performance was splendid, but other officers were less impressed. "Sir Henry Clinton showed himself the Soldier," one of them wrote, "but not the wise General . . . exposing himself and charging at the head of a few Dragoons." Lt. William Hale was "astonished at seeing the Commander of an Army galloping" wildly. The general's behavior dismayed Hale, who took offense at Clinton's "expressly forbidding all form and order" in attacking the hedgerow. Another account was less astringent, but still skeptical. During the fighting, "many instances of bravery was shown, perhaps too many by S[ir] Henry in person." It was not unusual for British generals to come under fire; without modern communications, they often had to be close to the action to maintain any command and control. Clinton had been in the fray before and had distinguished himself at Bunker Hill and on Long Island, but at Monmouth Courthouse, as Hale so acidly noted, his bravado imperiled his command at a critical juncture. On Perrine Hill, Washington had no reason to do anything similar.

Among the major generals, Lee, Stirling, Lafayette, Greene, and Steuben all had vital parts to play. Despite the controversy that has dogged his reputation since the Battle of Monmouth, Lee did not perform badly. He competently handled the vanguard in moving to contact, and he conducted a competent retreat across adverse terrain while facing superior numbers and the aggressive enemy cavalry. In the early morning, he did well to withdraw intact, as he did after the fighting at the hedgerow, and he fought satisfactorily at the hedgerow. Like the veteran officer he was, he variously took post at vantage points from which he could observe the action, took an active role in ordering artillery and infantry dispositions, and finally issued timely orders to pull back across the west morass. His mission had been to buy time for Washington to position the main army, and he had done so.

Lee also made his share of mistakes. Earlier in the day, he had not made his intentions clear to Scott and Maxwell and he did not maintain contact with them and Morgan. These failures were problematic. Lee's difficulty with Scott and Maxwell and, shortly thereafter, with Lafayette on the patriot right, stemmed partly from the poor state of Continental field communications, but these difficulties also stemmed from Lee's assumption that his subordinates would act according to his intentions without ensuring that they understood those intentions. The situation was analogous to Washington assuming Lee understood how badly Washington wanted the vanguard to hit Clinton. Still, once Lee realized the precariousness of his situation, he did not do badly. He was wise in ignoring Wayne's insistence on making a stand near the east morass. Lee's experience during the morning at Monmouth Courthouse demonstrated the maxim that once the shooting starts, generals have only limited control over events.

It is easy to disparage Lee. He was a not a likeable individual, and his abrasive personality and lack of social graces made him few friends. Unlike Washington, he was not an inspirational leader, and unlike Wayne, he saw little romance in war. His criticisms of the commander in chief have rankled not only many of his contemporaries, but also many historians. However, his conduct at Monmouth Courthouse does not deserve the obloquy many historians have directed at him. He was a competent general, though not a great one. Yet, among the historians who have faulted Lee's performance at Monmouth Courthouse, few (if any) have suggested what the general should have done differently. Should he have devised a specific plan before advancing? It is difficult to imagine how he could have, given the changing intelligence of the enemy situation. Did Lee fail to gather sufficient intelligence before advancing? If he had waited until Clinton's movements were clear, the redcoats would have been long gone and well out of reach of the blow Washington wanted Lee to strike. Should he have maintained better control of his command during the morning? Of course, but that would have been nigh impossible given the terrain and size of the battlefield, the fact that Scott and Maxwell had marched away from the action, the fact that Clinton was advancing with vastly superior numbers, and the necessity of making decisions on the spot. Should Lee have stood and fought east of the village as Wayne had wanted? If he had done so, Lee would have exposed his soldiers to mass slaughter. Could Lee have held a line east of the west morass? No historian has suggested, even remotely, where or how he could have. If Lee had tried to fight somewhere between Monmouth Courthouse and the hedgerow, Sir Henry would have been delighted. Critics have ignored these questions as well as the fact that Lee kept the vanguard in reasonable order, allowing major components of it to fight effectively at the Point of Woods and the hedgerow. Nor have most historians credited Lee with buying the time Washington needed to position his army on Perrine Hill. They have glossed over the fact that Lee retained the respect of many officers. It was only Lee's foolish insolence to Washington that led to the court-martial that doomed his reputation; it was not his performance on the battlefield.

The other major generals' actions were of varied importance. Stirling did well enough. The rebel "lord" deserved the credit he received for posting the main army on Perrine Hill as units came up and then opening artillery fire on the enemy. His timely action blunted British efforts to turn the Continental left and shattered Monckton's grenadiers. Stirling performed well; he faced straightforward circumstances that required little imagination. He served largely under Washington's eye and as a conduit for Washington's orders, and he was solid in the heat of battle. Greene showed himself a versatile officer. Shifting from his position as quartermaster, he happily assumed combat command. From Combs Hill, Greene's guns caused havoc with the British on the plains below. Steuben spent most of the campaign as an aide to the commander in chief and gathering intelligence. The Battle of Monmouth never tested him as a line commander; his final contributions were limited to relieving the exhausted Lee and bringing up the reserve late in the day.

The Monmouth Campaign found the Marquis de Lafayette still maturing as a leader. His problematic advance on 26 June did not result in a near catastrophe (as his adventure at Barren Hill had), but it certainly could have. His enthusiasm lacked the balance of experience belonging to more seasoned officers. But Lafayette was brave. He no longer had a defined role after Lee resumed command of the delaying force east of the west morass, but he remained forward as Lee held the hedgerow. Later, he held a small reserve behind Perrine Hill, and he maneuvered to discourage the British from moving on the patriot left. He was a willing warrior, and with a long war in front of him, his best days in command lay ahead.

Most of the army's brigadier generals saw too little action to allow for much observation or analysis. Only Wayne commanded in major combat, and his record is mixed. Wayne's penchant for fighting clouded his judgment early in the day; a Continental stand near the east morass, where he wanted to fight, would have invited disaster. Wayne's failure to send Morgan's rider on to Lee was a dereliction of duty. Wayne's men fought hard in the Point of Woods, but his role is obscure. Once the guards, light dragoons, and grenadiers crashed into the woods, Wayne's ability to control events was virtually nil, and leadership probably defaulted to the company and platoon levels—if even that was possible. (It was an example of how little a general could influence events in the midst of close combat). He did better later in the day. In the withdrawal toward the parsonage, Wayne's leadership matched his dramatic personality. Exposed to enemy fire and facing a determined attack, he shouted encouragement as the British closed in. Like Clinton and Monckton, Wayne attempted to rally the troops through personal example. The day certainly ended better for Wayne than it did for Monckton.

Regimental officers performed well. These men, from colonels down to ensigns, commanded the army's basic tactical units, from regiments down to platoons. They were responsible for motivating their troops, directing them in action, maintaining order, and engaging in personal combat. Motivation came in various forms. One rebel colonel, forming to meet the morning charge of the *16th Light Dragoons*, threatened to kill anyone who opened fire without orders—which was motivation of a kind. More frequently, however, officers exposed themselves to enemy fire to inspire their men. Steadying his 4th New York Regiment at the hedgerow, Col. Henry Beekman Livingston held his post after a musket ball smashed through his thigh. Cilley was a rousing leader, hailing his picked men as he gathered them to attack the *42d Foot*, then cheering them on for a final shot at the retiring highlanders. Staff officers Hamilton and Laurens stayed up front for all to see, Hamilton waving his sword, and both men lost their mounts to enemy fire. So did Aaron Burr as he led a regiment during Wayne's attack later in the day. These were brave officers who took leadership seriously, and, presumably, many other officers did as well.

Such competence among the regimental officers was the product of long experience. Steuben may have sharpened their skills in command and control, but by mid-1778, most of these officers were veterans. Historians have compiled the names of twenty-four of the colonels and lieutenant colonels, along with three majors and a captain, commanding the regiments or battalions of Lee's vanguard.

Two others cannot be identified with certainty. Ten of these officers received their commissions in state or Continental units in 1775, twelve in 1776, and two in January 1777. At least four of them had served in the Seven Years' War. This means that even the shortest-serving regimental and battalion commanders had at least a year and a half of active duty; most had well over two years. These officers had seen combat before, and their experience was evident at the Battle of Monmouth.

Thus, the battle revealed a growing competence in the patriot officer corps. Among Washington's generals, the test of combat produced examples of excellent leadership; it also saw examples of mediocre performance. Over the course of the day, Lee and Wayne each displayed instances of both. In a long day of combat, it is the rare general who has a faultless record of decision making. The important point is that senior Continental leadership was able to stabilize the situation and then fight a solid defensive battle. In this, they relied on a corps of regimental officers who were able to couple a grasp of command and control with the personal courage expected of combat leaders.

Despite the Continentals' ability to display many positive qualities at Monmouth Courthouse, the rebel military still had problems. Field communications remained a disability. The inability to identify units from a distance or to relay orders expeditiously brought Lee's morning attack to grief. Throughout the morning, too many of Lee's subordinates lacked orders or the means of getting them. In a battle of fixed positions or over limited ground, the lack of uniforms, colors (regimental or other flags), and enough staff officers to carry orders might not create major problems. They were not for Washington in the afternoon, when he fought from compact lines and sent out smaller units. Large maneuvers over time and space were a different matter. Lee had foreseen the problem. Without the ability to readily identify units, a commander would be in trouble. "Colours, Colours," Lee wrote well before Monmouth, "are the Life and Soul of Manoeuvering, and if ever Simplicity was necessary it certainly is for the Americans." There were some patriot colors at Monmouth Courthouse, but hardly enough to assist materially with the command and control of units across a major battlefield.

    The cavalry was another problem. The Continentals had barely enough horses to handle scouting duties, and, in their numbers and training, most rebel horse formations could not stand against the British. With no effective cavalry of his own, the enemy light dragoons were among Lee's greatest worries. Fears of being flanked by British light horse units compelled several shifts in position during the morning retreat, and at the hedgerow, the inability to counter the *16th Light Dragoons* was instrumental in forcing the patriot withdrawal. Nor did the rebels concentrate their available horse troops for the campaign. The dragoons of Maj. Henry "Light-Horse Harry" Lee, perhaps the most capable rebel horsemen, were foraging during the battle and never engaged. General Lee could have used them at the hedgerow, or they might have bolstered attempts to hit Clinton's baggage train. General Wayne believed Major Lee could have done some real damage had he been on hand. The cavalry was the weakest patriot combat arm in 1778, and it would remain so throughout the war.

    Finally, important weaknesses in Continental staff work were evident at Monmouth Courthouse. The chief problem lay in the control of detached corps. The failure to bring Morgan's riflemen into play was the most serious case in point. Conceding the difficulties inherent in eighteenth-century military communications, this business was still a major gaff. Once Washington had determined some kind of action, there was no excuse for his aides or another staff officer not to clarify Morgan's assignment. Yet, in the flurry of disjointed correspondence between Washington, Lee, Greene, and Morgan, no one thought to straighten out the matter. Nor, initially, did anyone pay adequate attention to what Lee's vanguard was doing early on 28 June. Washington received reports during the morning, but the flow of intelligence broke down, leaving him stunned to find Lee retreating. Lee, in turn, was not sure how closely Washington intended to support him. In fact, until the commander in chief confronted him, Lee was unsure of whether the main army would come any closer than Englishtown. Command and control of detachments is one of the most difficult tasks in the military catalogue, and in the ensuing years, Washington and his lieutenants would hone their skills. Three years after Monmouth, for example, in the Yorktown Campaign, major units moved separately but effectively over considerable distances. At Monmouth Courthouse, however, as at Brandywine and Germantown, staff capabilities necessary for such results were not yet in place.

On balance, the Valley Forge–Monmouth Campaign found the Continental Line formidable. It had improved its fighting qualities and support services, and its officers were more confident than in years past. In these crucial respects, if the Continentals had not come of age, at least they were *coming* of age. Washington was aware that the army still had critical weaknesses, but the commander in chief finally had a force approaching the "respectable army" he had wanted for so long. The army's proficiency would grow over the years; for the Continentals, the campaign was not so much a high-water mark as it was a part of the continuing evolution of a regular military.

In the immediate aftermath of Monmouth, General Dickinson was annoyed at his militia's quick dispersal and told Washington as much. Still, the militia only had left Monmouth Courthouse, not the war. Like the Continentals, the citizen-soldiers had learned a lot in more than two years of conflict. State authorities, however haltingly, gradually had improved New Jersey's militia laws and began to compel service. More militiamen served or hired substitutes, and those who fought gained invaluable experience. Over the course of the campaign, the militia was a vital element in the military equation. They had learned the arts of harassment and intelligence gathering. By hovering on Clinton's flanks, they forced the enemy to commit resources to security operations. Some militia units also fought staunchly in open battle. Monmouth showed the Continentals coming of age, and it did the same for the militia.

The ability of the Continentals and the militia to coordinate operations also was impressive. This was compound warfare. The effectiveness of the joint militia-Continental effort exemplified how an insurrectionary citizenry could, once its activities were linked with a regular army, confront a powerful enemy effectively. The British received a taste of this at Saratoga in 1777, and patriots would have been delighted to "Burgoyne"—a verb patriots invented for the occasion—Clinton in New Jersey. This, of course, did not happen. Burgoyne had marched to defeat over hundreds of miles of difficult country, leaving detachments of his army behind to guard his lines of communications. Clinton went a shorter distance over an established (if sometimes rudimentary) road network and had no need to deplete his strength guarding lines in his rear. Yet the campaign showed that the patriots credibly could threaten to repeat their performance against Burgoyne. Clinton's fate might have been quite different if his journey had extended another hundred miles beyond Monmouth Courthouse.

These improvements in the rebel war effort were matters of signal importance when viewed in the broader military context of the revolution. In open battle, the king's army still could face the Continental Army with a reasonable degree of confidence, even though the British realized the patriot regulars now were considerably more dangerous opponents than they previously had been. However, facing a war-wise populace at the same time was another matter. The New Jersey interior, with its hostile population and veteran militia, had become part of the quagmire that engulfed British armies whenever they strayed far from the American coast and *Royal Navy* support. Thus, the Valley Forge–Monmouth Campaign illustrated a problem the British never were able to solve.

In retrospect, the campaign, brief as it was, emerges as one of the more important of the struggle for independence. Even conceding that the Battle of Monmouth was a tactical draw and that Clinton successfully returned to New York, the campaign still made a significant political impact. After the defeats of 1777 and the harrowing Valley Forge winter, the campaign restored public confidence in General Washington and his Continental Army. Without that confidence, what chance did the revolution really have?

APPENDIX

"Order, Regularity, & Discipline": Waging War in the Eighteenth Century

by Joseph A. Seymour

By 1775, armies in Europe and North America had developed into complex forces organized around the infantry regiment. Artillery provided fire support. Mounted units performed reconnaissance, screened attacks and retreats, and added shock. Engineers and pioneers built and demolished fortifications and other works. Artificers repaired and maintained weapons and ordnance. Surgeons treated the sick and wounded. Civilian commissaries made, procured, and transported supplies and rations. All of them supported the foot soldiers, who usually dominated the battlefield.

Composition

The Continental Army and state militia generally organized their infantry regiments using the British model, with a colonel in command, aided by a lieutenant colonel, major, and regimental staff. A regiment had ten companies, including one light and one grenadier company. The light company consisted of the best shots, the cleverest, and the most agile in the regiment. These soldiers specialized in screening, skirmishing, patrolling, and scouting. Congress dispensed early on with the grenadier company, with its brawny shock troops who often formed the vanguard of assaults, and usually authorized nine companies. Each company carried equipment and additional ammunition in one or two wagons. When the situation called for the infantry to operate away from its baggage train, soldiers placed extra ammunition and essential items in their knapsacks. Most companies had a few women on their rolls. Although not officially in the army, they could draw rations, and sometimes pay, by performing various essential duties, including nursing the sick and wounded and laundering the soldiers' clothing. Captains and lieutenants directed the maneuver and fire of the platoons in their companies. Sergeants and corporals maintained unit cohesion in battle, assisted officers, and enforced discipline in the sections under their charge. Drummers, who ranked between corporals and sergeants, communicated orders in camp and battle.

Equipment

A soldier's basic fighting equipment was known as a stand of arms, which commonly consisted of a musket; a bayonet; a cartridge box of wood, leather, or tin containing between twenty-three and twenty-nine paper cartridges; and cleaning tools. A standard firearm of the period was the British Land Pattern musket. It fired a powerful load consisting of a 1-ounce lead ball propelled by nearly a half ounce of gunpowder. Its oversized barrel of about 0.76- to 0.80-inch diameter made it easier to load. A ball fired from a musket of this type could reach massed troops out to 300 yards. At 100 yards, it was accurate enough to hit an individual and powerful enough to penetrate a two-inch elm plank. Continental, state, and militia forces augmented existing musket stores with locally made copies of the Land Pattern and imported French, German, Dutch, and Spanish arms of similar bore sizes and ballistics. Soldiers also shouldered sporting (nonmilitary issue) arms of different calibers, sometimes retrofitted to mount bayonets. The lack of serviceable arms slowed augmentation and the integration of reinforcements. Furthermore, companies equipped with a mix of arms could not easily sustain fire, let alone mount effective bayonet assaults.

Both armies also issued rifles to light troops or recruited experienced riflemen who brought their own. The rifles usually followed two patterns: the short-barreled, large-bore Germanic or *Jäger* (hunter) rifle, and the long-barreled, small-bore Pennsylvania rifle. Less powerful than muskets, both were accurate to about 300 yards and took about one minute to load. Neither could mount a bayonet. In 1777, British Maj. Patrick Ferguson fielded an innovative breech-loading rifle that mounted a bayonet, but it saw limited service.

Tactics

The musket's capabilities shaped tactics. A trained soldier could fire three rounds per minute. After twenty-five shots, the piece became too hot to handle, and the accumulation of residual gunpowder (known as powder-fouling) required cleaning and slowed reloading. Regiments formed in line at close order, presenting a continuous front of muskets and bayonets to concentrate their fire and mass to maximum effect. Close ranks also enabled company commanders to keep their troops together and thus better control them. The soldiers easily could hear orders communicated by drumbeat and could support each other using linear tactics described in tactical publications such as the *Manual Exercise, As Ordered by His Majesty in 1764*. In 1778, the Continental Army introduced a system spelled out in the *Regulations for the Order and Discipline of the Troops of the United States*, nicknamed the Blue Book. Well-drilled companies could execute a variety of maneuvers to bring their firepower or bayonets to bear, unleashing simultaneous volleys with devastating effect, or firing alternately by platoon to sustain a running fire. Infantry usually closed to the optimal range of 40 yards for a killing volley before a bayonet assault. While battalions also could extend their intervals to optimize individual fire, volume rather than accuracy usually decided a battle's outcome.

Artillery on both sides organized as separate regiments and battalions but fought as detachments as needed. With a range of several hundred yards, 3-, 4-, and 6-pounder guns supported battalions in battle. With their slightly longer range, 8- and 12-pounders supported brigades, while larger guns with greater range operated from fortifications. Mortars fired exploding shells in a high arc to get over walls or other obstacles. Howitzers fired shells either directly at troops or in an arc. Artillerists and wagon teams were valuable assets. Commanders therefore often ordered crews that were about to be overrun by the enemy to disable their guns with spikes and mallets and abandon the weapons to save themselves and their teams.

Both forces also employed light dragoons, a type of mounted infantry. The scarcity of large horse breeds in America, the cost of transporting such mounts, and the uneven topography challenged the use of cavalry. Organized as regiments or separate troops, dragoons fought both mounted and dismounted and were armed with sabers, carbines, and, occasionally, pistols. Depending on time and terrain, both armies frequently detached light infantry, riflemen, artillery, and dragoons into separate battalions or combined them into corps or legions.

Fortifications

European and colonial governments constructed dozens of forts before and during the war to defend important cities, towns, and key points. Field fortifications included fort-like redoubts, arrow-shaped flèches, and crescent-shaped lunettes. These structures were built of large wicker cylinders, called gabions, which were filled with soil or rubble, and then reinforced by bundles of sticks called fascines, covered with soil and sod, and surrounded by moats. As time permitted, soldiers erected palisades (walls of vertical wooden stakes), placed fraises (sharpened stakes) at a slant on the inner surface of the moat, and laid an abatis (a network of felled trees with sharpened branches) to slow infantry assaults. For a portable obstacle, artificers would use a cheval-de-frise, which typically consisted of sharpened stakes projecting from a log or beam. To fortify harbor defenses and block rivers, engineers employed log booms connected with heavy chains and created the naval version of a cheval-de-frise by constructing rock-filled timber boxes bearing sharpened logs.

Technology dictated tactics, which in turn influenced formations. The contending forces frequently deviated from the standards prescribed by regulations or government allocations as they dealt with issues of personnel, materiel, and authority. Necessity and mission spurred the evolution of regulations, tactics, and equipment during the war. That was particularly the case for the new army of the United States. As the war progressed, American soldiers attained a high level of proficiency that earned the confidence of those they served and the respect of both allies and enemies.

> "The Course of human Affairs forbids an Expectation, that Troops formed under such Circumstances, should at once posses the Order, Regularity & Discipline of Veterans— Whatever Deficiencies there may be, will I doubt not, soon be made up by the Activity & Zeal of the Officers, and the Docility & Obedience of the Men. These Quali[ties,] united with their native Bravery, & Spirit will afford a happy Presage of Success, & put a final Period to those Distresses which now overwhelm this once happy Country."
>
> —George Washington, in an address to the Massachusetts Provincial Congress, 4 July 1775

BIBLIOGRAPHIC NOTE

PRIMARY SOURCES

The author consulted original diaries, letters, maps, orders, papers, and other records from the following archives, collections, and publications:

Amherst Papers. David Library of the American Revolution. Washington Crossing, PA.
André, John. *Andre's Journal*, 2 vols. Henry Cabot Lodge, ed. Boston, MA: Bibliophile Society, 1903.
Bloomfield, Joseph. *Citizen Soldier: The Revolutionary War Journal of Joseph Bloomfield*. Mark E. Lender and James Kirby Martin, eds., 2nd ed. Yardley, PA: Westholme, 2018.
Burton, I. F., ed. *James Pattison Papers, 1777–1781*. Woolwich, UK: Royal Artillery Institution, 1963.
Chase, Philander D., et al., eds. *The Papers of George Washington*, vols. 3–15. Charlottesville: University Press of Virginia, 1988.
Loftus Cliffe Papers. William L. Clements Library, University of Michigan. Ann Arbor, MI.
Clinton, Henry. *The American Rebellion: Sir Henry Clinton's Narrative of His Campaigns, 1775–1782, with an Appendix of Original Documents*. William B. Willcox, ed. New Haven, CT: Yale University Press, 1954.
Sir Henry Clinton Papers. William L. Clements Library, University of Michigan. Ann Arbor, MI.
Collections of the New York Historical Society for the Year 1872. The Lee Papers. New York: New York Historical Society, 1873.

Cushing, Harry Alonzo, ed. *The Writings of Samuel Adams*, 4 vols. New York: G. P. Putnam's Sons, 1907.

Downman, Francis. *The Services of Lieut.-Colonel Francis Downman, R.A., in France, North America, and the West Indies, between the Years 1758 and 1784*. F. A. Whinyates, ed. Woolwich, UK: Royal Artillery Institution, 1898.

Ferdinand J. Dreer Collection. Soldiers of the American Revolution Series. Historical Society of Pennsylvania. Philadelphia, PA.

Feilitzsch, Heinrich Carl Philipp von and Lieutenant Christian Friedrich Bartholomai. *Diaries of Two Ansbach Jaegers: Lieutenant Heinrich Carl Philipp von Feilitzsch and Lieutenant Christian Friedrich Bartholomai*. Bruce E. Burgoyne, trans. and ed. Bowie, MD: Heritage Books, 1997.

Frazer, Persifor. *Persifor Frazer: A Memoir Compiled Principally from His Own Papers*. Philadelphia, PA: privately printed, 1907.

Geography and Map Division. Library of Congress. Washington, DC.

George Washington Papers. Captured British Orderly Books. Library of Congress. Washington, DC.

Harvey, Edward. *The Manual Exercise, as Ordered by His Majesty in 1764. Together with Plans and Explanations of the Method Generally Practiced at Reviews and Field Days*. New York: W. Weyman, 1766.

Journals of the Continental Congress, 1774–1789, 34 vols. Worthington C. Ford et al., eds. Washington, DC: U.S. Government Printing Office, 1904–1937.

Henry Knox Papers. Massachusetts Historical Society. Boston, MA.

Krafft, John Charles Philip von. *Journal of Lieutenant John Charles Philip von Krafft*. New York: Arno Press, 1968 (orig. 1883).

Lafayette, Marie-Joseph Paul Yves Roch Gilbert du Motier, Marquis de. *Memoirs: Correspondence and Manuscripts of General Lafayette, Published by His Family*. London: Saunders and Otley, 1837.

———. *Lafayette in the Age of the American Revolution: Selected Letters and Papers, 1776–1790*, 5 vols. Stanley J. Idzerda et al., eds. Ithaca, NY: Cornell University Press, 1979.

Library of Valley Forge National Park. Valley Forge, PA.

MacGregor, Morris J. and Bernard C. Nulty, eds. *Blacks in the United States Armed Forces: Basic Documents*, 13 vols. Wilmington, DE: Scholarly Resources, 1977.

New Jersey Historical Society. Newark, NJ.

New Jersey Letters. Special Collections. Alexander Library, Rutgers University. New Brunswick, NJ.

New Jersey State Archives. Trenton, NJ.

Papers of the Continental Congress. Library of Congress. Washington, DC.

Papers of William Petty, Lord Shelburne. British Library. London.

Prince, Carl E., et al., eds. *Papers of William Livingston*, 5 vols. Trenton: New Jersey Historical Commission and Rutgers University Press, 1979–1988.

Proceedings of a General Court Martial. Held at Brunswick, in the State of New Jersey, by Order of His Excellency Gen. Washington . . . for the Trial of Major-General Lee. July 4th. 1778. Major-General Lord Stirling, President. New York: privately printed, 1864.

Reed, William B. *Life and Correspondence of Joseph Reed.* Philadelphia, PA: Lindsay and Blakiston, 1847.

Showman, Richard K., et al. *The Papers of General Nathanael Greene.* Chapel Hill: University of North Carolina Press, 1979.

Simcoe, J. G. *Simcoe's Military Journal: A History of the Operations of a Partisan Corps, Called the Queen's Rangers, Commanded by Lieut. Col. J. G. Simcoe, During the War of the American Revolution.* New York: Bartlett and Welford, 1844 (orig. 1787).

Smith, Paul H., ed. *Letters of Delegates to Congress.* Washington, DC: Library of Congress, 1982.

Steuben, Friedrich Wilhelm Augustine. *Regulations for Order and Discipline of the Troops of the United States.* Philadelphia, PA: Continental Congress, printed by Styner & Cist, 1779.

Syrett, Harold C. and Jacob E. Cooke, eds. *The Papers of Alexander Hamilton*, 27 vols. New York: Columbia University Press, 1961–1987.

SECONDARY SOURCES

Books

Anderson, Troyer Steele. *The Command of the Howe Brothers During the American Revolution.* New York: Octagon Books, 1972.

Barber, John W., and Henry Howe. *Historical Collections of the State of New Jersey.* New York: S. Tuttle, 1844.

Berg, Fred Anderson. *Encyclopedia of Continental Army Units: Battalions, Regiments and Independent Corps.* Harrisburg, PA: Stackpole Books, 1972.

Bilby, Joseph G., and Katherine Bilby Jenkins. *Monmouth Court House: The Battle that Made the American Army.* Yardley, PA: Westholme Publishing, 2010.

Billias, George Athan, ed. *George Washington's Generals.* New York: William Morrow, 1964.

Bodle, Wayne K. *The Valley Forge Winter: Civilians and Soldiers in War.* University Park, PA: Pennsylvania State University Press, 2002.

Bodle, Wayne K., and Jacqueline Thibaut. "Valley Forge Historical Research Report," Valley Forge National Historical Park, May 1980.

Callahan, North. *Henry Knox: George Washington's General.* New York: Rinehart, 1958.

Campbell, Charles, ed. *The Bland Papers: Being a Selection from the Manuscripts of Colonel Theodorick Bland, Jr.; To Which Are Prefixed an Introduction, and a Memoir of Colonel Bland,* 2 vols. Petersburg, VA: Edmund & Julian C. Ruffin, 1840–42.

Caruana, Adrian B. *British Artillery Ammunition, 1780.* Bloomfield, Ontario: Museum Restoration Services, 1979.

———. *Grasshoppers and Butterflies.* Bloomfield, Ontario: Museum Restoration Services, 1979.

Chadwick, Bruce. *George Washington's War: The Forging of a Revolutionary Leader and the American Presidency.* Naperville, IL: Sourcebooks, 2004.

Chernow, Ron. *Washington: A Life*. New York: Penguin Books, 2011.

Clary, David A., and Joseph W. A. Whitehorne. *The Inspectors General of the United States Army, 1777–1903*. Washington, DC: Office of the Inspector General and U.S. Army Center of Military History, 1987.

Davies, K. G. *Documents of the American Revolution, 1770–1783*. Colonial Office Series, Transcripts 1778. Shannon, Ireland: Irish University Press, 1973.

Elliott, Steven. *Surviving the Winters: Housing Washington's Army during the American Revolution*. Norman: University of Oklahoma Press, 2021.

Ewald, Johann. *Diary of the American War: A Hessian Journal*. Joseph Philip Tustin, trans. and ed. New Haven, CT: Yale University Press, 1979.

Ferling, John. *Winning Independence: The Decisive Years of the Revolutionary War, 1778–1781*. New York: Bloomsbury Publishing, 2021.

———. *The World Turned Upside Down: The American Victory in the War of Independence*. New York: Greenwood Press, 1988.

Garson, Noel B. *Light-Horse Harry: A Biography of Washington's Great Cavalryman, General Henry Lee*. Garden City, NY: Doubleday, 1966.

Glatthaar, Joseph T., and James Kirby Martin. *Forgotten Allies: The Oneida Indians and the American Revolution*. New York: Hill & Wang, 2007.

Golway, Terry. *Washington's General: Nathanael Greene and the Triumph of the American Revolution*. New York: Henry Holt, 2005.

Gruber, Ira D. *The Howe Brothers and the American Revolution*. New York: W. W. Norton, 1972.

Herrera, Ricardo A. *Feeding Washington's Army: Surviving the Valley Forge Winter of 1778*. Chapel Hill: University of North Carolina Press, 2022.

Hoffman, Ronald, and Peter J. Albert, eds. *Arms and Independence: The Military Character of the American Revolution*. Charlottesville, VA: United States Capitol Historical Society, 1984.

Houlding, J. A. *Fit for Service: The Training of the British Army, 1715–1795.* New York: Oxford University Press, 1981.

Huber, Thomas M., ed. *Compound Warfare: That Fatal Knot.* Fort Leavenworth, KS: U.S. Command and General Staff College Press, 2002.

Isaac, Rhys. *Landon Carter's Uneasy Kingdom: Revolution and Rebellion on a Virginia Plantation.* New York: Oxford University Press, 2004.

Jackson, John W. *With the British Army in Philadelphia, 1777–1778.* San Rafael, CA: Presidio Press, 1979.

Johnson, Victor Leroy. *The Administration of the American Commissariat during the Revolutionary War.* Philadelphia: University of Pennsylvania Press, 1941.

Johnston, Henry P., ed. *The Record of Connecticut Men in the Military and Naval Service during the War of the Revolution.* Hartford, CT: Case, Lockwood & Brainard, 1889.

Katcher, Philip R. N. *Encyclopedia of British, Provincial, and German Army Units, 1775–1783.* Harrisburg, PA: Stackpole Books, 1973.

Kurtz, Stephen G., and James H. Hutson, eds. *Essays on the American Revolution.* Chapel Hill: University of North Carolina Press, 1973.

Lender, Mark Edward. *Cabal! The Plot Against General Washington.* Yardley, PA: Westholme, 2019.

———. *The War for American Independence: A Reference Guide.* Santa Barbara, CA: ABC-CLIO, 2016.

Lender, Mark Edward, and Garry Wheeler Stone. *Fatal Sunday: George Washington, the Monmouth Campaign, and the Politics of Battle.* Norman: University of Oklahoma Press, 2017.

Lesser, Charles H., ed. *The Sinews of Independence: Monthly Strength Reports of the Continental Army.* Chicago, IL: University of Chicago Press, 1976.

Loane, Nancy K. *Following the Drum: Women at the Valley Forge Encampment.* Washington, DC: Potomac Books, 2009.

Lockhart, Paul. *The Drillmaster of Valley Forge: The Baron de Steuben and the Making of the American Army.* New York: Smithsonian Books, 2008.

Lossing, Benson J., ed. *The American Historical Record, and Repository of Notes and Queries.* Philadelphia, PA: John E. Potter, 1874.

Martin, James Kirby, and Mark Edward Lender. *A Respectable Army: The Military Origins of the Republic, 1753–1789,* 3rd ed. Malden, MA: Wiley, 2015.

Mayer, Holly A. *Belonging to the Army: Camp Followers and Community during the American Revolution.* Columbia: University of South Carolina Press, 1996.

Mazzagetti, Dominick. *Charles Lee: Self before Country.* New Brunswick, NJ: Rutgers University Press, 2013.

McKenney, Janice E. *The Organizational History of Field Artillery, 1775–2003.* Washington, DC: U.S. Army Center of Military History, 2007.

Morrissey, Brendan. *Monmouth Courthouse 1778: The Last Great Battle in the North.* Oxford, UK: Osprey Publishing, 2004.

Munn, David C. *Battles and Skirmishes of the American Revolution in New Jersey.* Trenton, NJ: Bureau of Geology and Topography, Department of Environmental Protection, 1976.

Narratives of the Revolution in New York: A Collection of Articles from the New-York Historical Society Quarterly, vol. 85. New York: New-York Historical Society, 1975.

Neimeyer, Charles Patrick. *America Goes to War: A Social History of the Continental Army.* New York: New York University Press, 1996.

Nelson, Paul David. *The Life of William Alexander, Lord Stirling.* Tuscaloosa: University of Alabama Press, 1987.

O'Shaughnessy, Andrew Jackson. *The Men Who Lost America: British Leadership, the American Revolution, and the Fate of the Empire.* New Haven, CT: Yale University Press, 2013.

Palmer, John M. *General von Steuben.* New Haven, CT: Yale University Press, 1937.

Pappas, Phillip. *Renegade Revolutionary: The Life of General Charles Lee.* New York: New York University Press, 2014.

Peckham, Howard H., ed. *The Toll of Independence: Engagements & Battle Casualties of the American Revolution.* Chicago, IL: University of Chicago Press, 1974.

Ramsay, David. *The History of the American Revolution*. Philadelphia, PA: R. Aitken & Son, 1789.

Rees, John U. *"They Were Good Soldiers": African-Americans Serving in the Continental Army, 1775–1783*. Warwick, UK: Helion & Company Limited, 2019.

Risch, Erna. *Supplying Washington's Army*. Washington, DC: U.S. Army Center of Military History, 1981.

Rossman, Kenneth R. *Thomas Mifflin and the Politics of the American Revolution*. Chapel Hill: University of North Carolina Press, 1952.

Salter, Edwin. *A History of Monmouth and Ocean Counties*. Bayonne, NJ: E. Gardner & Son, 1890.

Selesky, Harold E., ed., *Encyclopedia of the American Revolution*, 2nd ed. Detroit, MI: Thomson Gale, 2006.

Spring, Matthew H. *With Zeal and Bayonets Only: The British Army on Campaign in North America, 1775–1783*. Norman: University of Oklahoma Press, 2008.

Stone, Garry Wheeler, and Paul Schopp. *The Battle of Gloucester*. Yardley, PA: Westholme, 2022.

Stryker, William Scudder. *The Battle of Monmouth*. William Starr Myers, ed. Princeton, NJ: Princeton University Press, 1927.

Symmes, Frank R. *History of the Old Tennent Church*, 2nd ed. Cranbury, NJ: George W. Burroughs, 1904.

Taaffe, Stephen R. *The Philadelphia Campaign, 1777–1778*. Lawrence: University Press of Kansas, 2003.

Thayer, Theodore B. *The Making of a Scapegoat: Washington and Lee at Monmouth*. Port Washington, NY: Kennikat Press, 1976.

Walling, Richard S. *Men of Color at the Battle of Monmouth, June 28, 1778: The Role of African Americans and Native Americans at Monmouth*. Hightstown, NJ: Longstreet House, 1994.

Wilkin, W. H., ed., *Some British Soldiers in America*. London: Hugh Rees, 1914.

Wirth, Edna. *The British Encampment in Evesham Township*. Evesham, NJ: published by the author, 1987.

Wright, Robert K., Jr. *The Continental Army*. Washington, DC: U.S. Army Center of Military History, 2006 (revision forthcoming).

Periodicals

Cooper, Henrietta, ed. "Extracts from the Diary of Captain John Nice, of the Pennsylvania Line." *Pennsylvania Magazine of History and Biography* 16 (1892).

Danckert, Stephan C. "A Genius for Training: Baron von Steuben and the Training of the Continental Army." *Army History* 17 (1991).

Harris, Michael C., and Gary Ecelbarger. "A Reconsideration of Continental Army Numerical Strength at Valley Forge." *Journal of the American Revolution*, 18 May 2021. allthingsliberty.com/2021/05/a-reconsideration-of-continental-army-numerical-strength-at-valley-forge/.

Herrera, Ricardo A. "'[T]he zealous activity of Capt. Lee': Light-Horse Harry Lee and *Petite Guerre*." *Journal of Military History* 79 (2015).

McHenry, James. "The Battle of Monmouth." *Magazine of American History* 3 (1879).

"The Papers of General Samuel Smith." *The Historical Magazine* 2, no. 7 (1870).

Sivilich, Eric D., and Daniel M. Sivilich. "Surveying, Statistics, and Spatial Mapping: KOCOA Landscape Analysis of 18th-Century Artillery Placements at Monmouth Battlefield State Park." *Historical Archaeology* 48, no. 4 (2014).

Stone, Garry Wheeler, Daniel M. Sivilich, and Mark Edward Lender, "A Deadly Minuet: The Advance of the New England 'Picked Men' against the Royal Highlanders at the Battle of Monmouth, 28 June 1778." *Brigade Dispatch* 26, no. 2 (1996).

Zanine, Louis. "Brigadier General John Lacey and the Pennsylvania Militia in 1778." *Pennsylvania History* 48, no. 2 (1981).

Other Sources

Herrera, Ricardo A. "FOB Valley Forge: Washington's Armed Camp and the Schuylkill." Keynote, Eighteenth Annual Fort

Ticonderoga Seminar on the American Revolution, Ticonderoga, NY, 24 September 2022.

Olsen, Mark A. "Line and Rabble: Drill, Doctrine, and Military Books in Revolutionary America" Master's thesis, Joint Advanced Warfighting School, Joint Forces Staff College, 2018.

Sivilich, Eric D. BRAVO GIS files. Monmouth Battlefield State Park. Manalapan, NJ.

"Southern New Jersey and Delaware Bay." National Park Service, n.d. https://www.nps.gov/parkhistory/online_books/nj2/chap1.htm.

SERIES SOURCES

The following sources were used to prepare the entire "U.S. Army Campaigns of the Revolutionary War" series of monographs and are recommended for further reading:

Blackmore, David. *Destructive and Formidable: British Infantry Firepower, 1642–1765*. London: Frontline Books, 2014.

Peterson, Harold L. *Forts in America*. New York: Charles Scribner's Sons, 1964.

———. *Round Shot and Rammers*. Harrisburg, PA: Stackpole Books, 1969.

Rothenberg, Gunther. *The Art of Warfare in the Age of Napoleon*. Bloomington: University of Indiana Press, 1980.

THE AUTHOR

Mark Edward Lender has a PhD in American history from Rutgers University, and he is now professor emeritus at Kean University, from which he retired as the vice president for academic affairs. He is the author or coauthor of thirteen books, including *Cabal! The Plot against General Washington* (2019) and *Fort Ticonderoga, the Last Campaigns: The War in the North, 1777–1783* (2022). His scholarship has won various awards, among them the Society for Military History's Distinguished Book of the Year (2017) and a Distinguished Writing Award from the Army Historical Foundation, both for *Fatal Sunday: George Washington, the Monmouth Campaign, and the Politics of Battle*. He was a finalist for the prestigious George Washington Literary Prize and is a recipient of the Richard J. Hughes Award, the highest honor bestowed by the New Jersey Historical Commission for contributions to state history. He lives in Richmond, Virginia, with his wife, Rutgers University librarian emerita and author Penny Booth Page.

The author wishes to thank the CMH editorial board who gave their time and attention to three drafts of this manuscript and series editor David Hogan for his advice and encouragement. Penny Booth Page carefully edited the drafts and offered sound critiques. Cartographer Matt Boan did a first-rate job in drafting maps to accompany my text, and Margaret J. B. McGarry provided incisive editorial support. All of the above have my sincere thanks and appreciation.